THE KINDNESS OF STRANGERS

A HISTORY OF THE LORT SMITH ANIMAL HOSPITAL

FELICITY JACK

SPINIFEX

In many areas of Indigenous Australia it is considered offensive to publish photographs of Aboriginal people who have recently died. Readers are warned that this book may contain such pictures.

Spinifex Press Pty Ltd
504 Queensberry Street
North Melbourne, Vic. 3051
Australia
women@spinifexpress.com.au
http://www.spinifexpress.com.au

First published by Spinifex Press, 2003

Cover and book design by Deb Snibson, The Modern Art Production Group
Made and printed in Australia by McPherson's Printing Group

National Library of Australia
Cataloguing-in-Publication data:

Jack, Felicity.
The kindness of strangers : A history of the Lort Smith Animal Hospital.

Bibliography.
Includes index.
ISBN 1 876756 39 X.

1. Lort Smith Animal Hospital - History. 2. Veterinary
   hospitals - Victoria - Melbourne. I. Title.

636.0832099451

Lort Smith Animal Hospital

Lort Smith Animal Hospital is a charity devoted to:

- Quality care for sick, injured and stray animals
- Caring for animals of those with limited means
- Promoting responsible pet ownership
- Fostering in our community an awareness of animals and the benefits they bring

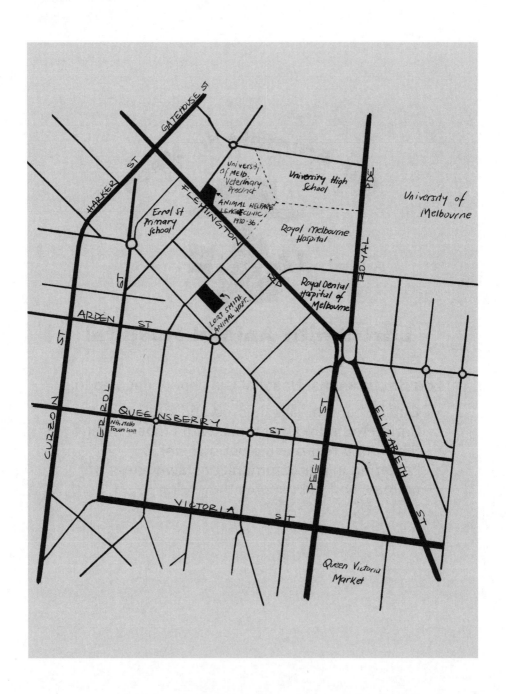

CONTENTS

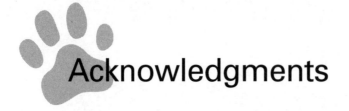

Acknowledgments

Thank you to all the members of the Board of the Lort Smith Animal Hospital, and especially Dr Gerald Clarkson, Mrs Virginia Edwards, Dr Alan Lawther and Mr David White. Thanks also to past members of the Board who provided me with assistance and information: Mrs Pat Patience, Mrs Phyllis Taylor and Mr David Alsop.

Many past and present staff members have given invaluable help. These are too numerous to mention but include: Mrs Joan Sturzaker, Mrs Jeannie McKenzie, Mr Michael Curry, Mrs Chris Farrell, Dr Harold Pook, Dr Patrick Cheah, Mr Steven Isaac, Mr Vladimir Kovak, Ms Katy Kennedy and Mr Peter Brown. Past staff members include Dr Cimati, Dr Richard Nemec, Dr Don Tynan, Mrs Carol Hutchins, Mrs June Price and Mrs Pat Jarrett.

Assistance has also been received from the RSPCA and the Lost Dogs' Home. Jeanie Campbell provided me with some invaluable information, and I also received help from Mrs Angela Darling, Mr John Montgomery Dale, Mrs Jillian Gengoult Smith, Mr Tom Lyle and Mrs Heather Ronald.

Thank you to Mrs Bet Moore and Ms Janet Graham for their help with preparation of the manuscript, and Ms Irene McCallum and Mr David Alsop for their graphic design.

Thanks to *The Age*, the *Herald and Weekly Times*, the *Leader Community Newspapers*, Keith Bedford of Snapshots, Graham Cornish and Norman Wodetski for allowing us to publish their photographs, and the Hotham History Project for allowing me to use photographs previously scanned for the publication of *Faithful Friends*.

Special thanks to all the staff at Spinifex Press, particularly Belinda Morris, Maralann Damiano, Susan Hawthorne, Elana Markowitz and Deb Snibson.

Introduction

The Lort Smith Animal Hospital has a proud history. It grew out of the Animal Welfare League, established in 1927 with the main purpose of raising money to help disadvantaged animals and their owners. Initially the funds were distributed between two existing animal welfare institutions, the Lost Dogs' Home and the Rest Home for Horses run by the Victorian Society for the Protection of Animals which is known today as the RSPCA.

The depression years brought increasing distress to the population of Australia, and at a time when assistance was increasingly looked for by the poor to help in treatment of pets the only body which was set up to provide such a service to needy animal owners was forced to close its doors. This was the veterinary clinic for poor people which had been running at the University of Melbourne to give training to the vets of the Veterinary School. This had failed to attract sufficient students to make it viable. One of the vets attached to the clinic, Dr Bordeaux, had the foresight to suggest to the recently founded Animal Welfare League that they should seek assistance from the University of Melbourne to take over the running of the clinic and thus maintain this vital service. This was generally known as the Animal Welfare League Clinic. Several years later, in 1935, the League set up the Lort Smith Animal Hospital on its present site.

The League's vision was that the hospital would provide a place where people with limited financial resources could obtain veterinary treatment for their animals. While this altruistic goal may have been to reduce unnecessary suffering by ill and injured animals, the hospital has also helped to reduce the anxiety, pain and grief felt by the thousands of people who have had to accompany their animals to the hospital. Thus, throughout its long history the hospital has been committed to serving both animal welfare and social welfare – a unique vision.

Animals, particularly dogs and cats, have many roles in families and in society. Those who have been able to grow up with one or more pets can consider themselves fortunate. Many consider that the care afforded to animals is a reflection of the development of a community as a sophisticated and caring civilised society. Perhaps the work of the Animal Welfare League and its Lort Smith Animal Hospital is one of the reasons why Melbourne can be promoted as one of the world's most liveable cities!

This history of the Lort Smith Animal Hospital acknowledges the roles played by many people at different stages of the hospital's development. In the beginning it was the leadership, drive and determination of a group of women concerned for animal welfare. The history records the many struggles to obtain the resources: funds to establish and operate the hospital without favoured support from government, such as providing tax deductions for donations. It was also a struggle to employ and retain veterinarians when there were so few in Victoria before the first graduates appeared from the re-established University of Melbourne Veterinary School in 1967.

This is a rich history, often coloured by battles over differences of opinion arising from tensions between very determined people. If a reader of this history wants to see whether the struggle of the people concerned has been worthwhile I would recommend that they pay a visit to this state of the art centre for the treatment of animals, the Lort Smith Animal Hospital, at 24 Villiers Street, North Melbourne. It is an outstanding Melbourne institution providing a high standard of treatment to animals. What makes it different from other such institutions is that it has maintained its long tradition of providing medical care for animals of those members of the community who are disadvantaged, thus providing an invaluable service to those for whom pet ownership would otherwise be beyond their means.

Professor Ivan Caple,
Professor of Veterinary Medicine and
Dean of the Faculty of Veterinary Science
University of Melbourne.

Preface

It is the attractive old hospital building, built in 1935 and then named the Lort Smith-Lyle Hospital, that passers-by see first as they walk along Villiers Street. It is now known as Lyle House. As one looks through the wide gates which lead to the car park the new state-of-the art hospital, opened in December 2000, comes into view. The old leading to the new – this is indeed symbolic of the hospital and what it means to the history of animal welfare in Victoria.

The Lort Smith-Lyle Hospital which opened in 1936, *The Animal Lover book of the Animal Welfare League*, 1940.

The Animal Welfare League of Victoria (AWL) opened a clinic in Flemington Road, Parkville in 1930. It was replaced with a hospital on its present site in Villiers Street, North Melbourne in 1936. Both clinic and hospital provided affordable treatment for the animals of those unable to pay the fees of private vets, a need heightened by the Great Depression years.

The hospital was commonly known as the Animal Welfare League Hospital in its early years although, until a falling out between Lady Lyle and the League in 1942, its official name was the Lort Smith-Lyle Hospital. In the 1950s and 1960s it was commonly referred to as the 'Lorty'; today it is most often known as the Lort Smith Animal Hospital, the Lort Smith for short. The hospital is still run under the auspices of the Animal Welfare League of Victoria.

Mrs Mima Andrew, c. 1940, *The Animal Lover book of the Animal Welfare League,* 1940.

Detail of hospital signage c. 1940, *AWL scrapbook.*

Mima Andrew, vice-president of the League, described the clinic in the early 1930s and this was quoted in a newspaper cutting found in one of Mrs Lort Smith's scrapbooks. With some changes the same story could be told today. Dollars have replaced shillings, a computer-operated appointment system has replaced numbered cards, and today's hospital welcomes clients from all economic classes – not just the impoverished. And ragged children wearing grandfather's trousers would be an unlikely sight. Today's clientele is likely to have a higher proportion of elderly pensioners and fewer unemployed because of socio-economic changes.

An odd assortment of people-some young, some middle-aged, and some very old and tired. They struggle up the wide path singly and in groups, to the Animal Welfare Clinic. Each carries or leads an animal of some sort. Sometimes it is a frisky 'pom' with a touch of mange, which does not seem to affect his spirits. At other times it is a dejected greyhound with distemper or a limping horse led slowly, patiently, by his owner. Two ragged boys – one wearing his grandfather's trousers, judging by appearances – carry a magpie, which looks very woebegone. They tell a long story about 'Mag' getting into a pot of paint in the back yard. 'Mag' squawks dismally, apparently in confirmation of their tale. A strange elderly woman in black satin and bath slippers, with festoons of coffee lace across her bosom, carries a tabby cat wrapped in a piece of red table cloth. Puss has a sore ear, and she is 'telling the world about it.' A shabby man with kindly eyes nurses a fox-terrier puppy with wonderful gentleness. The puppy whimpers softly. One of his legs dangles pathetically. The children have run over him with a scooter, the man explains. His voice is full of concern as he tells his story. One and all they file into the big square courtyard, and line up in turns for their numbered admission cards. They pay their shillings and drift over to the seats on the grass to await their turn.

... Just before I leave I look at the rows of uncomplaining little creatures who are so utterly dependent on one's good will, and at the faces of their owners, so many of whom are out of work and 'up against it.' But despite their troubles they find time to trudge along carrying Digger or Spot, and to wait patiently until the veterinary surgeon eases his suffering.

An example of how little things have changed is illustrated by this article which appeared in the Lort Smith newsletter of October 1981, over twenty years ago. It could have been at almost any time during the existence of the hospital, except for the names.

Sunday at the hospital – 21st June, 1981

Melbourne's suburbs are still asleep on the drive to the hospital, but at Lort Smith things are already in hand before 8.30 am. Chris is doing the waiting bays, Rose is already hard at work in the Cattery, and Sandy and Steven are finishing cleaning the kennels. Mr McD. is already waiting with 'Dobey'.

The waiting rooms fill rapidly. There is an emergency in Surgery 2 – a blood transfusion is required. 'Fat Mumma', a cat, is brought in by her owner; she has a tuberous growth on her lip.

An ambulance call comes in from Pascoe Vale South. A man has found a sick cocker spaniel which has made a nest for itself in a pile of garden rubbish. The dog has a collar and a disc on but won't let the man near it. While his wife is telephoning the Hospital the dog gets up and runs away. We tell Mrs H. to ring us back quickly if the dog reappears, and to try to confine it.

Mrs C. rings in. Her son is getting up out of a sick bed to bring in her very sick dog. Can we put them through quickly, please? We oblige.

We hear Dr Cimati's voice coming over the public address system, so the emergency in Surgery 2 is over and now there are three vets seeing patients – Dr Cimati, Dr Brooks and Dr Cameron. There is a constant stream of people in front of 'Cookie' at the reception desk, and the two new waiting rooms are constantly full.

It is the time of year for Defender poisonings, and these cases take time to treat.

We have enquiries for kittens, which are hard to come by at this time of the year. Lucille goes down to the Cattery to see what we have – we have only two young cats which are very nervous and will need to stay a week in the Hospital to settle down.

The male corgi-cross which we sold this morning has escaped in the Fitzroy Gardens. The new owners have spent two hours looking for him. The Lost Dogs' Home is alerted.

We hear again from Mr and Mrs H. The sick cocker spaniel is now under the house. Chris goes out in the ambulance and after some trouble manages to bring it in. It is very sick and it is wearing a Broadmeadows disc. We will be able to find its owner in the morning.

The waiting rooms are still full at 5 pm. When Nasser arrives the day staff go home after a busy day, and the evening staff carry on the good work.

But not everything has stayed the same. The hospital has undergone several metamorphoses over the years, and as the hospital has enlarged it has required significant modifications. Two major upgrades have taken place, the first in 1960 and another in the early 1980s. In the mid-1990s the Board decided to completely rebuild the hospital. This happened at the end of the 1990s and the new building was opened at the end of the year 2000. One important innovation has enabled the Lort Smith to deliver state of the art treatment: the intensive care unit (ICU). This has proved invaluable in some of the touch and go cases which arrive at the hospital: patients such as Max Bakita who had been badly injured when hit by a car early one morning. She was treated in the new hospital in 2001 and written up in the hospital's summer newsletter under the heading 'I will survive':

The hospital wasn't open yet. Thankfully behind the closed doors dedicated staff commence their day earlier. Max was rushed into the Intensive Care Unit and assessed. A grim picture emerged of multiple life threatening injuries, each potentially fatal in their own right. Abdominal haemorrhage goes to the back of the queue as the lungs collapse and her breathing falters.

Skilled, experienced people put their competency into action. Like any other emergency room you may imagine. I.V. catheters, fluids and E.T. tubes are used in quick succession. A chest drain goes in quickly and a suction system gets to work, racing to keep up with her leaky lungs. Even inflated, her lungs have had too much trauma to work well, so she must go on to a ventilator. True life support. At this point, like any other badly injured person, she depends on a machine to keep her alive. Many things are going on, body systems struggling to keep going. Pain, shock, blood loss, tissue trauma over nearly all her body, all creating a host of acronyms. Simple letters suggesting deadly outcomes. MODS, SIRS, ARDS, DIC. Just another day for the ICU but it would prove to be a long one. Minute by minute, hour by hour, the challenges increase and are met.

Max was too ill to move. The machine that breathed for her was working well, but when she came off it she fell away very rapidly. The ICU nurse had already over-stayed her 12 hour shift. We have no funds or contingency plans for another ICU nurse. The ICU is a trial service and though it has proved successful and popular there it is not a foregone conclusion that another nurse will be employed to provide consistent ICU treatment seven days a week. Let alone 24 hours a day. Steve, another highly qualified nurse has been a strong supporter of the ICU trial. He was available and willing to nurse Max through the night.

Saturday and Max is able to come off the ventilator; after 26 hours on life support her lungs are able to function. Brain injuries become a concern and her heart seems to have been injured as well, beating irregularly. The abdominal haemorrhage seems to have settled which is just as well, no chance to operate with her grip on life so fragile. Sunday and the tense hours have turned to days. Her heart settles,

Max Bakita survives!
Hospital newsletter,
Summer 2001.

but looking into her eyes there is no-one home. Nothing but a little rise in heart rate when the owners visit. Things look grim. Janine and Steve alternate shifts as Max stabilises. Come Monday Max is looking about, too weak to raise her head, but keen to eat ... Max went home the following Wednesday.

Expansion of hospital staff and premises has brought a huge increase in clients: during 2001 the Lort Smith Animal Hospital carried out 34,500 consultations and 8500 surgical procedures. It looked after 800 stray dogs, and the cat shelter took in 2350 cats. There were 680 wildlife admittances. This compares with 5000 sick and injured animals which attended the Animal Welfare Clinic in the twelve months ending 4 March 1931.

At the request of the Board, this book was written to record the history of the Animal Welfare League of Victoria and the Lort Smith Animal Hospital. They felt that it was important that an account of the events, and particularly the people who have contributed so much, should be kept for posterity.

Lort Smith Animal Hospital Board members, 2003.

Left to right: Mr Ian Davey, Mrs Susie Palmer, Mrs Virginia Edwards, Mrs Susi Edwards, Mr David White, Ms Maggie Allmand, Dr Judith Slocombe, Dr Gerald Clarkson, Mr Rick Macdonald and Dr Alan Lawther.

The League has survived because of the strong vision of its founders and the determination of Board members, past and present, to maintain the strength of this vision. Many of the supporters of the League have showed indomitable spirit and perseverance and just two of the many stories about the refusal to take 'no' for an answer are included here. One is of Lady Lyle and Mrs Lort Smith relentlessly pursuing Victoria's Premier, Thomas Holloway, through state parliament in an attempt to get a state government grant. Then in 1949 Mrs Lort Smith was outraged to be told by Melbourne's Town Clerk, Mr Wooton, that he would not give the hospital a grant because he considered it to be 'an unnecessary organisation'. So she complained by letter to the Lord Mayor, sending it to his personal address. The hospital got its grant.

One of the challenges of writing this history has been the lack of detail about many of the events and the people who have been involved in the seventy-five years covered. The minute books of the early years are sparse and cover more of the fundraising and social activities of the League than the setting-up and running of the clinic. Minute books have been supplemented with newspaper accounts, cuttings from scrapbooks, often undated and with the source unattributed, records of meetings of the Australian Veterinary Association and a few surviving scraps of correspondence.

Frequently people's names have been only partially recorded and in the early days a woman rarely used her own given name, usually being known by that of her husband. Sometimes no given name has been recorded, and precise identification has been difficult. It has similarly been difficult to track the different committees of the Australian Veterinary Association, of which the Victorian Veterinary Association is a branch. In the 1980s there was also the Veterinary Practitioners Association with the Metropolitan Practitioners Board being a sub-branch of that. Also confusing is the Victorian Society for the Protection of Animals, often shortened to VPA. Around 1927 it became the Society for the Prevention of Cruelty to Animals. Both names continued to be used for many years. In 1956 the name was officially changed to the Royal Society for the Prevention of Cruelty to Animals.

Although a good many years have passed since the League decided to become involved in the treatment of animals, many of the same needs, obstacles and challenges remain. Perhaps the one societal change which has worked in the League's favour has been the resurgence of a laissez-faire economy with greater emphasis on the benefits of competition. As a result the veterinary profession has relaxed the sometimes stringent restrictions it had been able to impose on the League in the past. These included strict regulations about advertising and the types of treatment the hospital was allowed to offer.

Some themes recur time and again. They include the need for close communication between the Board and the staff, the difficulty of running a service without government funding and the fact that donors are unable to claim a tax deduction. But the most consistent and outstanding theme is the commitment and generosity of a huge number of people who share the vision of improving conditions for animals.

From small beginnings

The Animal Welfare League of Victoria was set up primarily to raise funds for charity, its main task being to organise Animal Welfare Week. This was seven days of intense fundraising throughout both town and country Victoria, coordinated by a group of women. It started in 1927 at a meeting held at the Toorak home of the politician Mr (later Sir) Henry and Mrs Ruth Gullett. The meeting was arranged at the request of a number of women representing the Lost Dogs' Home and the Victorian Society for the Protection of Animals under the leadership of Mrs Norman Brookes. The money raised by Animal Week during 1927 was distributed between the Home (£442) and the VSPA (£704). Some of the other women involved on the committee were Mrs Arthur Payne (vice-president of the Lost Dogs' Home), Mrs Lort Smith (also a committee member of the Home), and Mrs E. H. Davidson, the wife of the aide-de-camp to Victoria's Governor, Lord Somers.

Dame Mabel Brookes was born in 1890. She married Norman Brookes in 1911. He was a famous tennis player and in 1907, he was the first Australian to win at Wimbledon. His later work as a tennis administrator took him on many overseas trips where Mabel, who accompanied him, mixed with the rich and famous. Norman was also employed at the Australian Paper Mills and was made chairman in 1921.

Mabel Brookes believed that women were discriminated against in public life, and twice stood for parliament. In 1943 she stood as a 'Women for Canberra' candidate, and in 1952 she contested the state seat of Toorak for the Electoral Reform League. According to the Australian Dictionary of Biography she 'attracted few votes but much public attention'. Her platforms included free education from kindergarten to university, a health service to reduce infant mortality, reform of mental hospitals, and housing for the poor.

She was appointed CBE in 1933 and DBE in 1953 for her services to hospitals and charity. After her death on 30 April 1975 Sir Robert Menzies paid tribute to her as 'one of the most remarkable women of her time', possessed of 'a beautiful organising mind'.

Mrs Norman Brookes,
The Animal Lover book
of the Animal Welfare
League, 1940.

On 21 April 1927 the society magazine *Table Talk* mentioned that Mrs Norman Brookes had been elected president of the Animal Week committee and continued that this was very fortunate as

> *she makes a big success of anything she undertakes. Her secret is that she leaves nothing to chance, but has such a grip of the object she is at the moment interested in and personally supervises all arrangements.*

The article also described Mrs Brookes as a leader of the younger society matrons. She had a big and influential following, and her large circle of friends always rallied round when she called on them for help.

Louisa Lort Smith, née Montgomery, was born in Sale in 1875 and died on 16 July 1956. She was one of twelve children. Her father, William Montgomery, had been a soldier in the 50th Regiment, a career he gave up to come to Victoria in 1841 when he was nineteen. He is said to have had a strong pioneer spirit, and settled on an estate named 'Childhood Heart' near Sale where he bred cattle. From the age of eight Louisa drove a small goat cart around the paddocks looking for lost and abandoned calves to bring in to the homestead for care. The children were brought up on the estate enjoying the excitements of an active outdoor life. One favourite occupation was going out on horseback after rain with stock whips to kill snakes. On one day they killed eighty. Growing up on a cattle station made Louisa sensitive to the cruelty perpetrated on animals through branding and slaughtering methods. This influenced her dedication to the prevention of cruelty to animals in all its forms.

In 1885 the family business failed and the family moved to Caulfield.

A description of Mrs Lort Smith shows a formidable, determined woman of great presence:

short and stout, she was more like a hansom cab than a fashion plate in build. She had intense blue eyes, and a stare from her could stop any animal beater in his tracks. When she got up to speak everyone listened. (Margaret Hazzard writing in *Parade*, June 1974)

Louisa's marriage certificate recorded her profession as pianist, but she was also a dance teacher. She taught many well-known people including the Australian Prime Minister Harold Holt and Dame Mabel Brookes. Her marriage in 1925 gave Mrs Lort Smith sufficient financial independence to allow her to devote her time to the welfare of animals. She travelled overseas to England, Scotland and America three times, visiting animal welfare institutions and publicising the work of Melbourne's Animal Welfare League.

Mrs Lort Smith's ashes were buried under the grass plot in the Lort Smith Animal Hospital in accordance with her wishes. A bird-bath was erected in her memory, and also a memory pool, neither of which still remain. During the recent rebuilding of the hospital her ashes were dug up and carefully looked after until they could be safely reburied under the grass. In December 2001 her nephew and niece, John Montgomery Dale and Angela Darling, unveiled a plaque which they donated to the hospital in her memory.

Mrs Lort Smith, *The Animal Lover book of the Animal Welfare League*, 1940.

Mrs Angela Darling and Mr John Montgomery Dale, Photo: Lort Smith Animal Hospital.

On 1 May 1928 a meeting held at Mrs Payne's home, 'Scotsburn', Toorak Road, Toorak, was to have significant implications for animals throughout Victoria. Thirty-nine people attended the meeting, which formally approved the Objects and Rules of the Animal Welfare League. The objects were:

- to promote and improve the welfare of animals generally
- to take such steps as may from time to time be deemed expedient for the purpose of raising funds to carry out the objects of the League
- to undertake any business or thing which may either directly or indirectly conduce to any of the objects of the League
- to aid, support and subscribe to any Society, Institution, Association, or body of persons having objects altogether or in part similar to those of the League
- to register the League under the Companies Act or any other Act if thought advisable.

All thirty-nine people present signed the document, and according to the Rules these people comprised the first committee of the League, with power to add to their number.

The Rules allowed the committee to elect one or more patrons and an Executive consisting of a president (Mrs Yvonne Davidson), two or more vice-presidents (Lady Elder, Mrs W. R. Napier and Mrs Harold Clapp), an honorary secretary (Mrs James Purves) and an honorary treasurer (Mr R. Treloar). At least five other members could be appointed to the Executive and these were the members of the original animal welfare committee; Mrs Lort Smith, Mrs Payne, Mrs Andrew, Mrs Fred Krcrouse and Miss Marion Montgomery.

Mr Lort Smith drew up the rules of the League.

Charles Lort Smith was born in Bendigo in 1856. His father had been a gold buyer for the Bank of Australasia in Bendigo in the heyday of the gold industry. Charles spent many of his boyhood years in England and was educated in Hereford. He practised law for many years with the firm Nunn Smith and Jeffreson at 448 Collins Street. He was solicitor for the Victorian Racing Club for forty years and for the Victoria Amateur Turf Club for many years. He drafted the Australian rules of racing and was a recognised authority on racing law. He had lived for a long

time at 184 George Street, East Malvern before his marriage on 19 December 1925 to Louisa Montgomery at St George's Church of England Church in Malvern. Charles was aged sixty-nine, Louisa was fifty, and neither had been previously married. Charles died on 6 April 1931 from encephalitis lethargica after being ill for three weeks. He was buried in Sale, Gippsland.

The Executive had the power to add to their number and had full control of administration. An annual general meeting was to be held every year in April or May at which a new Executive was to be elected, with previous members being eligible for re-election.

The people who attended the meeting were:

Mr Lort Smith, Australasian, 17 October 1925, Newspaper Collection, State Library of Victoria.

(Mrs) Yvonne Davidson
(Mrs) L. E. Lort Smith
(Mrs) Mima Andrew
(Mrs) E. M. Krcrouse
M. Napier
E. Douglas Stephens
Esme Frankenburg
Lucy Stogdale
Mollie Neil
Mary Littlejohn
Nellie King
J. Saunders
(Mrs) A. M. Payne

Mollie E. Menzies
Mary H. Keep
(Mrs) Vivien Noel Clapp
M. K. B. Morley
I. S. Brogden
F. Howard Clark
Nellie Bagot
Gretta Affleck
R. French
Marjorie Kimpton
Mrs Barry Thomson
(Mr) R. R. Treloar
Sadie Purves

Valerie A. Purves
Jean Fink
Amy Nicholas
Ruth Whiting
Margaret B. Elder
Mrs Arch. Currie
Marion Montgomery
G. Reynolds
Marion Boothby
Jean McHarg
Nancy Stephens
(Mr) C. Lort Smith

(The names are recorded as they were written, except where the person's title is known, and this has been added in brackets to denote gender.)

The Argus reported the meeting on the following day, and gave details of the speech made by Mrs Davidson, in which she emphasised the necessity for:

approaching the subject of animal welfare with a sound, common-sense attitude, free from any silly sentimentality. Animals ... should be our helpmates and friends, and our aim in this work is to alleviate cases of distress among every class of animal, and to educate people to treat all animals in a humane way. In time to come, with the co-operation of the Education departments, we hope to have special lecturers sent to teach animal welfare and the law of kindness in every State School in Victoria.

The Argus also listed the proposed fundraising events including a ball on 6 July (tickets 12s 6d). Various sub-committees were formed to organise different activities. Vivien Clapp chaired the group running the annual ball at the Embassy, a public ballroom at 100 Collins Street. She was extremely well known for her theatrical presentations, in which she had at first performed but later produced. For many years she held the record for being the most successful money-raiser for charity. Her skills were used to organise entertainment at some of the League's functions. Two of Vivien's grand-daughters, Virginia Edwards and her cousin Susi Edwards, inherited her altruism and both are currently Board members.

Mrs E. H. Davidson, *The Sun*, 8 February 1930, Newspaper Collection, State Library of Victoria.

Other organised activities included bridge parties, raffles and a children's fancy dress party. As a result £350 was donated to the Lost Dogs' Home and £207 to the Horses Rest Home (run by the VSPA).

Although the objects of the Animal Welfare League were sufficiently broad-based to give it scope to develop in a variety of ways, the early meetings were entirely devoted to fundraising. The minutes of the League's meetings give no indication that it was considering extending its activities. This was to change.

The University of Melbourne's veterinary school had run a veterinary clinic where people, unable to afford treatment from vets in private practice, could have their animal treated for a registration fee of one shilling. This clinic gave third-year students experience in both dissecting and treating animals. However, in 1928 the school was forced to cease its undergraduate teaching role because it failed to attract enough students to make it economic, so the clinic was faced with closure.

Mrs Vivien Clapp, *Table Talk*, 22 October 1931, *Virginia Edwards' scrapbook*.

Facilities in the University of Melbourne Veterinary School, late 1920s, *Unidentified newspaper, AWL scrapbook.*

Dr Bordeaux was attached to the University of Melbourne veterinary school and he was also an honorary veterinary surgeon at the Lost Dogs' Home. He would therefore have been well acquainted with the Lort Smiths – Mr Lort Smith was the chairman and Mrs Lort Smith a committee member – as well as other members of the Animal Welfare League. Mr Lort Smith also acted as a solicitor for the University of Melbourne. Reluctant to see the facilities of the university stand unused, and recognising that the clinic did meet a real need for people who could not afford private veterinary treatment, particularly now the economic depression was deepening, Dr Bordeaux approached the League with a request that it consider taking over the clinic in partnership with the university.

Dr Bordeaux was born in Paris in 1871 and educated at the University of Paris. He served three years in a cavalry regiment and when he was living in Paris he was well known as an amateur rider. He then spent five years in the East Indies. In 1898 he arrived in Victoria and began to study veterinary science at the Melbourne Veterinary College. He graduated in 1902 whereupon he established his veterinary hospital at 'Cora Lynn', Mount Alexander Road, Moonee Ponds. He obtained his doctorate from the University of Melbourne Veterinary School in 1928, and lectured in canine diseases at the Veterinary School until it closed. In later life he specialised in equine surgery and was a brilliant diagnostician. He was a member of the Victoria Racing Club and sole veterinarian to the Moonee Valley and Maribyrnong Racing Clubs.

As well as the Lort Smiths, many of the members of the Animal Welfare League were supporters of the Lost Dogs' Home. However, the Home was increasingly losing favour with members of the League; Charles and Louisa resigned from the Lost Dogs' Home committee in 1929. There were two main reasons for disillusionment with the Home. First, the Home was allegedly involved with the sale of dogs to the University of Melbourne, and it was suggested that it was indirectly implicated in vivisection. In fact it was the Melbourne City Council who had an agreement to provide the university with dogs but because the Lost Dogs' Home was the designated place for the dogs to be sent on collection it was unwillingly involved. Second, there was dissatisfaction with the way the Home treated its animals.

Dr Bordeaux first approached the League's Executive at a meeting on 9 August 1929 at 'Woranga', the home of the Lort Smiths. There were only six members present – the president, Mrs Norman Brookes was sick and apologies were sent by Mrs Krcrouse and Mrs Clapp. The chair was taken by one of the vice-presidents, Mrs Payne, and the other members present were Mrs Andrews, Mrs Morley, Mrs Lort Smith, Mrs Purves and Miss Marion Montgomery. (Miss Montgomery was Mrs Lort Smith's sister, and a well known dancing teacher. She held annual balls which were attended by Melbourne's young elite, and these functions became important fundraising events for the League.)

Dr Bordeaux had to sit through the main topics of the meeting – all to do with fundraising. A ball was to be held at the Embassy Ballroom during Caulfield Cup Week, and Mrs Arthur Payne was to give an afternoon party at which it was hoped new members would be attracted to the League. Arrangements included the details of raffles for which Mrs Payne donated six pairs of silk stockings, Mrs Lort Smith a case of champagne, and Miss Bapt a doll. Mrs Lort Smith promised to look after the publicity and speak over the wireless about the aims and objects of the League.

Dr Bordeaux with Mr Williams (dispenser), Mrs Lort Smith and Miss Montgomery at the opening of the clinic, *The Sun,* **11 March 1930,** *Newspaper Collection, State Library of Victoria.*

It was only at the very end of the meeting that Dr Bordeaux was able to speak, but the minutes record simply that 'a discussion took place as to the advisability of opening a clinic – Dr Bordeaux has expressed the opinion that this was very necessary'.

It was decided to canvass the opinion of members at an 'at home' given by Mrs Payne later in August. Dr Bordeaux was asked to put forward his suggestions and after much discussion the members decided that the clinic be tried for one year at a cost of not more than £500 and if successful it would be carried on.

A planning meeting was held on 2 October 1929 at 'Kurneh', the home of Mrs Brookes. Mrs Brookes, Mrs Lort Smith, Mrs Andrew, Mrs Purves, Mrs Krcrouse, Mrs Dougharty, and the Misses Montgomery, Greene and Lempriere were present. Dr Bordeaux was their guest. He outlined his proposal as to how an agreement could be reached with the University of Melbourne. It was agreed that Mrs Brookes and Mrs Lort Smith should have an interview with Mr Bainbridge, university registrar, to discuss and clarify arrangements. Clearly this interview was successful because on 28 October 1929 a sub-committee was formed to oversee the running of the clinic. It was made up of Mrs Lort Smith (convener), Mrs Davidson, Mrs Andrew and Mrs Payne. Mr Lort Smith agreed to act as legal adviser, and Mrs Norman Brookes promised to assist in any way she could.

The same meeting discussed the allocation of the £575 raised during the year. This was raised mostly by the Animal Week October Appeal, and came from a variety of sources including a ball run by Miss Montgomery, a further ball at the Embassy, bridge parties and raffles. Donations of £150 were made to the Lost Dogs' Home and the SPCA, the remainder going toward the running of the proposed clinic. It was agreed that £500 be put aside for the clinic and deposited in the bank. Also at this meeting Mrs Purves resigned as honorary secretary, though promising to remain on the committee and to assist the League. She was replaced by Mrs Lort Smith.

Further discussion with the university and the SPCA resulted in setting-up a coordinating committee comprising two members of the League, two members of the SPCA and two members of the university. Mrs Lort Smith and Mrs Fred (Essie) Krcrouse – the wife of another Melbourne solicitor and barrister – represented the League.

The Animal Welfare League Clinic on the corner of Park Street and Flemington Road,
Herald, **11 October 1935,** *Newspaper Collection, State Library of Victoria.*

Agreement was reached with Mr Bainbridge that the lower room of the veterinary school, with attendants and what medicines were there, would be at the committee's disposal. It was made very clear in the League's agreement with the university that no research was to be done at the clinic. The Animal Welfare League was extremely opposed to any research on animals. Indeed, one wonders whether the League was not somewhat hypocritical in entering into a relationship with an institution which it heartily condemned for taking dogs indirectly from the Lost Dogs' Home for research purposes, a procedure which the Home also condemned while being implicated against its will. The League used the issue of the sale of dogs to the university to attack the Home, while at the same time entering into a business relationship with the university.

Clinic to hospital: 1930-1939

This newspaper article by Mima Andrew, a continuation of that printed in the preface, concludes the graphic picture of how the early clinic operated.

Little Creatures of the Poor – At the Animal Welfare Clinic:

A table stands on a verandah. No time is wasted by the veterinary surgeon, but each patient is handled with wonderful gentleness and skill. His white-coated assistant hurries hither and thither with bandages, dressings and hypodermic injections for cases of distemper. There are very few 'complaints.' The cats protest most, but the dogs are more philosophical. They seem to realise it is 'all for their own good.'

A man aged nearly 70 years talks in an undertone to his dog. He looks up and smiles. 'How do ye like my Rover?' he inquires. 'He is well bred, you can see that,' he adds with pride. Rover is a fine dog, foxy-red in colour, with wide intelligent eyes; but he has not much breeding, poor dear, although his manners are excellent. He is quite well now, but some weeks ago he arrived at the clinic almost at death's door; he was too ill to walk home, and his owner was too feeble to carry him. A helper sent the dog home in her car and earned undying gratitude of his owner. He is thanking her now with tears in his eyes.

'He's all I've got,' he says tremulously, and one catches a brief glimpse of an averted tragedy.

A smart Baby Austin ambulance, the gift of a sympathiser, now makes transport easier. Driven by volunteer helpers, it buzzes about Moonee Ponds, Footscray and Camberwell, carrying animals which are too ill to walk or animals whose owners have no friends willing to give them a 'lift.'

At one side of the courtyard is the dispensary, with rows of bottles and a kindly dispenser, who always has time to give some comforting advice. There is a big jar of dog biscuits, and another of oatmeal biscuits, labelled 'For Hungry Children.' Sad to say, these are often needed.

Graham Lowry and his dog make the front page of *The Sun* following the opening of the Animal Welfare League Clinic, *The Sun*, 11 March 1930, *Newspaper Collection, State Library of Victoria.*

Lord Somers opened the clinic on 8 March 1930. He was accompanied by his wife, Lady Finola Somers. One hundred and fifty guests were invited to afternoon tea, and the VSPA joined the League in catering for the event. The clinic was opened to the public immediately after the opening ceremony.

Mrs C. Lort Smith, *The Argus*, 8 March 1930, *Newspaper Collection, State Library of Victoria.*

At first the clinic opened for two afternoons a week, but this was later extended to three. For the first year or two it was funded jointly by the Animal Welfare League and the VSPA but the VSPA withdrew when financial problems meant they could no longer afford to contribute. It seems that the VSPA began to have difficulty raising funds because many of their supporters switched their allegiance to the more fashionable League.

Much of the clinic's work appears to have taken place out of doors. The main diagnosis and treatment area was a patch of grass, with two tables set up for examining the animals. Presumably the tables would have been moved under cover in bad weather.

The Executive enjoyed a close relationship with Lady Somers in the early 1930s. She agreed to their request that the clinic should be named after her although this seems to have been a mere formality as it continued to be called the Animal Welfare League Clinic. A meeting was convened at Government House on 10 September 1930 to plan for Animal Week to be held in the last week of October. Lady Somers presided by virtue of her status, although the League's president, Mrs Norman Brookes, was also there. Other members who attended this meeting were Mrs Mima Andrew (vice-president), Lady Lyle, Mrs Arthur Payne, Mrs Krcrouse, Mrs Purves, Mrs Lort Smith, Mrs U. J. Nicholas, Mrs Lawrence, Miss Montgomery, Miss Chirnside, Miss Doris Moffatt, Miss Millear, Mrs Crook and Miss Harvey.

At the next meeting Lady Somers offered to hold a bridge party at Government House to raise funds for Animal Week. This did not proceed, the likely reason a disagreement between herself and the Lost Dogs' Home.

Several contentious issues existed between the members of the League and the Lost Dogs' Home including the way in which the Home provided care for the dogs. Things came to a head in mid-1930 when Lady Somers, Patron of the Lost Dogs' Home, tried to make suggestions to a Board meeting about ways to improve treatment. Her words were badly received – in fact her supporters, including Mrs Lort Smith, publicly maintained that members of the Board had treated her with rudeness. A major confrontation between Mrs Lort Smith and Mr Morley, honorary secretary of the Home, took place at the Home's annual general meeting on 8 November 1930 and the argument received a good deal of publicity in the press. The animosity between the two organisations continued for many years.

Protocol demanded that Lady Somers should not side with one group of people over another, and there was public suggestion that Mrs Lort Smith had influenced Lady Somers in her confrontation with the Lost Dogs' Home. So the offer of the bridge party at Government House had to be withdrawn to offset claims that Lady Somers was favouring the League. It is likely that this argument also led to Mrs Payne, vice-president of the Lost Dogs' Home, resigning from the League.

The main role of the League's Executive during these years continued to be the organisation of Animal Week and other social events which took place throughout the year. The running of the hospital was left to a house committee and in July 1933 Mrs Lort Smith, who had held the position of honorary secretary since 1929, was given the title of hospital directress, with full power to make decisions. She continued in that position until 1941.

THE HOSPITAL COMMITTEE.
From Left: Miss Jean Johnstone, Mrs. Walsoe, Miss Doris Moffat, Mrs. C. L. Smith, Lady Lyle, Miss Nance Armstrong and Miss Marion Montgomery.

A house committee meeting held in September 1936 consisted of Mrs Lort Smith, Mrs Walsoe, Mrs Trathan, Miss Fraser, Mrs Semple, Miss Norwood, Lady Lyle, Miss Montgomery, Miss Armstrong and the Secretary.

Lady Frances Isobel Clare Lyle, née Millear (1870-22 May 1949), was noted for her animal welfare work. She joined the Animal Welfare League in or around 1930. She was married to Thomas Ranken Lyle (1860-1944) a physicist and mathematician. He was Professor of Natural Philosophy at the University of Melbourne (1889-1915) and a Commissioner of the State Electricity Commission from 1919. He worked closely with Sir John Monash. In 1918 Lady Lyle was appointed CBE in recognition of her untiring work on behalf of the Australian fighting units during the Great War.

Lady Lyle was not only a regular worker at the Lort Smith-Lyle Hospital, she also cared for lost and stray dogs in the family home at 'Lisbouy', Irving Road, Toorak. She had little time for people who did not care for their animals and is reputed to have used a blunt tongue to reprimand any client who she felt was not looking after an animal properly.

According to an article in the *Sun News Pictorial*, written by the columnist 'Prudence' (23 November 1939), Lady Lyle had been engaged in this philanthropic work for nearly forty years. She had originally started with around half a dozen strays but as the number increased she built special facilities for them in the grounds of 'Lisbuoy', including a lethal chamber that was, according to one of Lady Lyle's obituaries, the first to be built in Australia.

Clare Millear, later Lady Lyle, *Photo courtesy of Thomas Lyle.*

When 'Lisbuoy' was sold in 1939 Lady Lyle retained the cow paddock of the old home (over an acre of land with an outlet to Maple Grove) and built her own dogs' home called the Mercy Home. The grounds were planted with Japanese and other flowering trees which made a picturesque setting for a five-roomed villa. The main purpose of the home was the painless destruction of injured and aged animals, and it operated until 1946.

Nan Greville, wife of the hospital's first permanent vet, knew Lady Lyle in the 1940s and she told Board member Gerry Clarkson of her memories of her. Lady Lyle didn't care what she wore or looked like, and was always very earnest in her endeavours, shunning the limelight and always working 'behind the scenes'. She knew what she wanted and wouldn't put up with any nonsense. She could also be very gentle. When Nan's husband Ron was a prisoner of war she sent Nan some charming and delightful letters (quoted in chapter three).

The minutes of the September 1956 Board meeting, when the Lort Smith Memorial Appeal was being planned with a view to extending the hospital, recorded that Lady Lyle's name should be commemorated in a suitable manner once the work was finished. This did not occur until 2001 when the original hospital building was called 'Lyle House'.

Lisbouy, home of Lady Lyle, *Photo courtesy of Thomas Lyle.*

27

Lady Fairbairn joined the Board in December 1932 and took over the presidency in 1935. Mrs Lort Smith was made a Justice of the Peace on 23 January 1934, and this enabled her, together with another Justice, to authorise severely injured animals to be destroyed.

Mrs Lort Smith and Lady Lyle worked tirelessly for the hospital. They, and others from the League, particularly Lady Fairbairn, were also heavily involved in campaigning on behalf of animal welfare on a wide variety of issues and causes, and also took every opportunity to educate the public about animal care through newspaper and magazine articles. Here is one example from a newspaper in Mrs Lort Smith's scrapbook. More about the League's campaigns is contained in chapter twelve.

HORSES NEED
CARE IN HEAT

Should Be Watered Four Times a Day

HAT IS ESSENTIAL

"DURING the hot weather drivers should give special attention to their horses," said the secretary of the Animal Welfare League, (Mrs. C. Lort Smith) yesterday.

Horses which are working in the sun need water four times a day."

If no troughs were handy, Mrs. Lort Smith suggests that any householder would supply a bucket of water.

"Horses are very fond of green pea shells," she added. "Thousands of pounds of shells are wasted, and it would be a simple matter for housewives to wrap them in paper and ask tradesmen to mix them with the midday feed for their horses.

Save Animal's Head

"Hats for horses working in the sun are essential, and can be bought very cheaply. They will prevent the sun striking directly on the animal's head," she said.

Mrs. Lort Smith also suggested that dishes of water should be placed within easy reach of birds, dogs and cats.

In May 1933 it had been agreed that the hospital needed a person who could take more administrative responsibility for its running, and Mrs Lort Smith and Lady Fairbairn agreed to contribute £2 per month toward the funding of this position for a period of one year. Mr P. Wingrove was appointed secretary on 26 July 1933 with a salary of £300, plus £50 a year as allowance for the upkeep of the ambulance – to include servicing and garaging. This arrangement did not last long, and at a meeting on 24 August 1933 it was decided to replace Mr Wingrove. No reasons were recorded. Mr Wilfred Ryan was appointed but, at the suggestion of the solicitor, Mr James Purves (the husband of a Board member and a former partner of Mr Lort Smith, but whose role in this affair is unclear), it was agreed that 'the appointment must not be officially announced'. There were no unfair dismissal laws in those days: the employer held all the power to hire and fire, with no avenues for appeal. There is no indication that Mr Wingrove was even given the opportunity to put his case before the Executive. It is not known when or why Mr Ryan ceased to be employed.

It is not surprising that the clinic received some critical comment. An article appeared in *The Sun* on 10 February 1934 alleging that the coir mats under the tables on which

'Horses need care in heat', *Article from unidentified newspaper, AWL scrapbook.*

the animals received attention at the clinic were not disinfected, that pigs were kept in a pen next door to the room in which four men and twelve women worked, and that there was only one drinking trough for all the horses, including those carrying infections. Mr Ryan, the League's secretary, strenuously denied all these claims in both *The Star* and *The Sun*. He agreed that there was only one drinking trough for horses, but said that this was not used by horses with strangles (a highly contagious equine disease). However, he did point out that, because the premises were owned by the University of Melbourne, the League was at a disadvantage since it was unable to improve conditions by making any alterations.

Board member Mrs M. Walsoe and volunteer Miss Kindellan lift a patient from the new hospital ambulance, mid 1930s, *AWL scrapbook*.

The Australian Veterinary Association (AVA), keen to protect the livelihood of its members in private practice, also opposed the operation of the hospital. It had powers to regulate the operations of the League, and took every opportunity to do so. The AVA's role in the development of the hospital is covered in more detail in chapter nine.

The hospital did not operate at a profit, and therefore continued to rely on fundraising, both to survive and to expand. One way in which the hospital could extend its service was to provide transport for people who would not otherwise be able to make their way to Parkville. Therefore Mrs Lort Smith took the initiative of writing to Mrs W. H. Crook of Auburn Road, Auburn in April 1930. Mrs Crook was administering the estate of her late brother, Mr George Bills, and Mrs Lort Smith asked for a donation of a motorcycle ambulance for the clinic. Mrs Crook visited the clinic and handed over a cheque for £100 for a Baby Austin ambulance.

In September 1930 Mrs Crook was invited to a meeting of the Executive held at 'Kurneh', the home of Mrs Brookes, where she was thanked for her gift and shown the newly purchased ambulance. The main aim of the meeting was to plan the forthcoming Animal Week, and Mrs Crook handed over a further donation of £100. Gifts of a handbag (Mrs Payne), a case of champagne (Mrs Lort Smith) and two pairs of silk stockings (Miss Moffatt) were provided for a raffle.

In January 1934 *The Age* reported that the League's work had increased considerably, and that during the year 6729 dogs, 2599 cats, 475 horses, 201 birds, and 50 other animals including hares, rabbits, rats, a native cat and a camel had been treated. Over the past five years a total of 75,000 animals had been treated. However, Mrs Lort Smith was quoted as saying that the work was 'at present restricted because of the lack of public support'. The clinic relied heavily on voluntary helpers, particularly ambulance drivers, and the work appealed to young girls who had just left school. This quote from the 'Melbourne Letters' in Sydney's *Sun and Guardian* in July 1938 shows that volunteering was not all plain sailing!

> *All the society girls who can drive a car and handle an elephant turn out and do a spot of volunteer driving of the Animal Welfare Ambulance, which calls for and delivers its patients. But there is a severe test before they are accepted. One girl I knew had to park a sick parrot on one trip, and induce a baby elephant to enter the doors on her return.*
>
> *When I asked her how she did it, she said 'It's just will-power.'*

Volunteers grouped around the League's smart ambulance are Mrs Gange, Miss Pat Kirby, Miss M. Thomas, Miss V. Wilkinson, Miss Dorothy Banks, Miss Rosemary Mathew, Miss Judy Laing, Mrs Keith Halley, Mrs O. Gratian (who drives the ambulance) and Miss Diana Foster-Woods, *Table Talk*, 22 June 1939, *Newspaper Collection, State Library of Victoria.*

There were several reasons why the League needed to consider opening its own premises. As already mentioned, it had no control over how the university-owned premises could be used or modified; its services were beginning to outgrow the facilities, and there was no permanency in the arrangement. (The university did give notice to the League to vacate the property because it required it for its own purposes, but this was not until the new hospital building was nearly completed.) All the same the League's decision to open a hospital was not taken easily, but was given more urgency by the Lost Dogs' Home announcing that it was to open its own hospital. This led to much acrimonious public debate. Letters to the press were concerned about the duplication of services and queried why the two organisations could not get their act together. Then there was a public exchange of letters in *The Sun* in October 1935 between the Reverend Wilfred Lansdell Clarke, president of the Lost Dogs' Home and chaplain at Melbourne Grammar School, and Lady Lyle about which institution could claim to be the 'first' animal hospital. Lady Lyle promised to donate £10 to the Home 'upon proof that the Lost Dogs' Home had continuously functioned as a hospital since February 1913'. Four letters were published on the subject but there was no resolution to the debate.

At this time the Lost Dogs' Home was keen to amalgamate with the Animal Welfare League, and was prepared to make considerable concessions to facilitate this. The League however, would not entertain such an arrangement and insisted on maintaining its autonomy. The League enlisted the support of Dr Albiston of the Australian Veterinary Association to intervene with the Lost Dogs' Home and argue against its building a hospital. The Home however, was determined to proceed with its plans, and its hospital was opened by the Governor-General, Sir Isaac Isaacs, on 27 May 1935.

Less than two weeks before the opening of the rival hospital Mrs Lort Smith told the Board that she had found an excellent site in Villiers Street, North Melbourne on which to build a hospital, and by the next Board meeting on 29 May, she had already had discussions with the architect, Leighton Irwin, about drawing up plans. The suggested site was ideal for an animal hospital – close to the university and the

Veterinary Research Institute, within easy distance of the city centre and close to public transport. Trams stopped only a few hundred yards away, but since these did not allow animals as passengers the proximity of North Melbourne railway station was important.

Francis Leighton Irwin was a specialist in hospital architecture and had designed the Epworth and Prince Henry's Hospitals. He was president of the Victorian Institute of Architects 1931-33 and president of the Royal Melbourne Technical College 1936-38. The plans were drawn up quickly. The president, Lady Fairbairn, laid the foundation stone on 13 November 1935 and the hospital was opened officially five months later, on 16 April 1936, by Sir James Barrett, Chancellor of the University of Melbourne.

Modern Animal Hospital

HERALD 4/2/36

The court-yard of the new Animal Hospital, now being erected for the Animal Welfare League.

So within a year, a second treatment centre for animals came into being, both located in the same suburb.

The hospital had a frontage of 70 feet (21 metres) and a depth of 200 feet (60 metres). The front was faced with cream-coloured bricks, the roof was Chinese blue and the window shutters green. The operating theatre was a replica in miniature of a hospital theatre, and an X-ray plant was planned but not installed until 1938.

Building a hospital at this time was made possible only through the generosity of Lady Lyle who contributed £5000 toward it – an

Hospital for Pets

The Animal Welfare League carries on its work in Villiers Street, North Melbourne, in much the same way as do our public hospitals. Animals are called for, treated and returned to their owners for the most part sound in body and mind.

The Lort Smith and Lyle Hospital in Villiers Street, North Melbourne. Up to date and we equipped, it can hold its own with any other hospital in Australia.

Patients arriving at the hospital for treatment.

The Animal Welfare League ambulances tour every suburb collecting and returning animals, sick and well, to their owners. Mrs Phil Williams, Miss Ivah Perry and Miss Amelia Nathan are seen just about to start out on a trip.

Mrs Simon Fraser and Miss Connie Fraser, voluntary workers at the hospital examining a patient.

Secretarial work. Miss E Sansome acting as admitting officer.

Inspecting patients well on the way to wards recovery.

A permanent job is held down by Miss Marion Thomas, who is a qualified chemist. Her work is full time and extremely interesting.

The most modern of X-rays is used to assist in the diagnosis of complaints.

TABLE TALK
August 17, 1939
Page IV.

Hospital for Pets, *Table Talk,* **17 August 1939,** *Newspaper Collection, State Library of Victoria.*

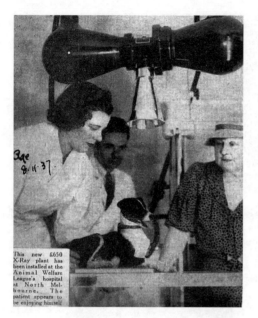

This new £650 X-Ray plant has been installed at the Animal Welfare League's hospital at North Melbourne. The patient appears to be enjoying himself

Mrs Lort Smith and Simon Fraser with X-ray equipment, the person on the left is unknown. *The Age* 8 November 1937, *AWL scrapbook.*

enormous sum in those days. She was an unassuming person who did not want to draw attention to herself and refused an invitation to lay the foundation stone. Nevertheless she did allow her name to be used in connection with the hospital, which, for some years after completion, was called the Lort Smith-Lyle Hospital. A further example of her reluctance to receive publicity was her request that her name be removed from a publicly circulated paper she had written on the care of dogs because, to quote from the minutes, 'she wishes to be less in the limelight. The publicity she gets is sometimes rather too much for her she feels'.

In 1936 Mrs Lort Smith and Miss Marion Montgomery went on a six-month trip to England and America, returning in September. Mrs Lort Smith told an interviewer from the *Herald* that she had been most impressed with the X-ray equipment being used in American hospitals. She had visited Chicago, Buffalo, New York, Boston and St Louis and had found wonderfully equipped animal hospitals in all these centres, which were either privately owned or run in conjunction with veterinary schools. She was determined that the Animal Welfare League would acquire the very best of such equipment, which she valued at around £350. It was installed at the hospital in 1938, a further gift of the George Bills estate.

The same staff who had worked at the clinic continued to work at the new hospital, but new members were appointed to cope with the additional workload. Dr Bordeaux remained the veterinary surgeon from the opening of the clinic until 1937, assisted by Mr Wilson. They were replaced by the hospital's first full-time vet, Mr Greville, in July 1937. On 22 September 1930 Mr Williams was appointed as the first anaesthetist.

Simon and Nell Fraser were to become well-known staff members at the hospital and an extract from *The Age* on 15 August 1935 gives details of their appointment:

It was announced that Mr and Mrs Simon Fraser of Inverness Scotland have been appointed superintendent and organiser of the new hospital. On completion of the building they will permanently reside there.

Their appointment had been negotiated by Mrs Lort Smith who had met them whilst she was travelling overseas and visiting different animal welfare establishments in 1934. Simon Fraser, according to Dr Richard Nemec, a vet who became very friendly with Simon, had no formal veterinary qualification but learnt a good deal of his veterinary skill from Dr Bordeaux whom he described as both father figure and professional mentor. Dr Bordeaux gave his surgical instruments to Simon Fraser, who in turn passed them on to Richard Nemec.

Dr Donald Tynan has these recollections of the Frasers, whom he knew several years later when he was working at the hospital between 1965 and 1968:

Simon Fraser [was] slightly hunched, tanned skin, high brow topped by sparse silver hair, spectacles, white coat, slight build, a piece of cord always ready for a muzzle or snare and a pair of scissors. Gentle, considerate, loving his Nell.

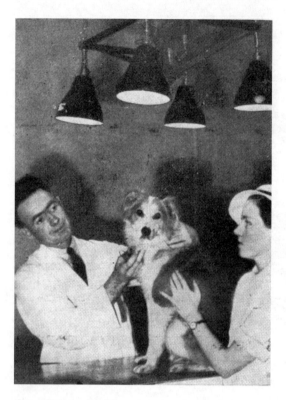

Nell [was] a very feminine ageing Scottish lady, colourful dressing, brooch, operating in the confined space of the pharmacy – a small sliding door into the surgery, a counter outside for the clients. It was she who mixed the carboys of Zinc Cream with chloretone, dispensed foul lime sulphur for mange, and myriad small paper envelopes of anything else.

Simon was immensely knowledgeable if you invited him by asking. I recall him always remarking-on completing yet another shaving of yet another summer eczema case, 'that it will give it a lot of relief.' Under Simon's tutelage I came to recognise persistent right aortic arch syndrome in puppies as they walked through the door.'

Several times, Simon told me, animals had been thrown over the locked gate in the dead of night. Many times was he knocked up by persistent and panicking 'emergencies'.

Simon Fraser examining dog, *The Animal Lover* book of the Animal Welfare League, 1940.

The hospital's first full-time vet, Ron Greville, had recently graduated from the University of Sydney, and had worked for a short time in Townsville before deciding to make the move to Melbourne in July 1937. Ron told Board member Gerry Clarkson in an interview in 1999 what it was like starting at the Lort Smith as a sole vet without much practical experience:

I had to undertake procedures and perform operations I had not seen done before and without other professional assistance. I had to be innovative and resourceful. Simon Fraser was most helpful and skillful. I found that the veterinary text books available did not meet my requirements and so resorted to buying and using medical text books as guides and calling on the assistance of medical practitioners.

By the end of 1938 Ron's relationship with the League's Executive was under strain. There were two points of contention – his professional autonomy and his private practice. An additional clause was written into his contract that the hours between 10 am and 6 pm were for the exclusive work of the League, and any private practice undertaken outside these hours should not occur on hospital premises and hospital equipment should not be used. Ron had been a captain in the Australian Army Veterinary Corps since 1936, so was certain to be called up in the event of war. Further conditions were therefore added:

In view of existing conditions the option of a second year not to be considered, also in the event of hostilities and Mr Greville being called away to military duties, his salary to cease from the day he leaves the League to the day of his return within the Year. Vacation to be observed along the lines of the Hospital's usual routine. Namely:- Two weeks of the Year on full pay and if so desired one further week without pay.

Ron married Nan (Nancy) Mellor, a voluntary worker at the hospital, in January 1939. They had one son prior to Ron's leaving for the war in 1940.

Fundraising remained a major part of the League's activities during the 1930s, and the annual Animal Week continued to provide a focus. In 1933 a shop was opened in the city. *The Argus* reported that the League's shop at 258 Collins Street would be opened from Monday 24 to Friday 28 October and would have:

a window display which would include a tiny Pekingese valued at one hundred guineas; a champion red Persian cat and kittens; a Royal Siamese cat, of legendary fame, and a litter of three tiny puppies with a cat foster-mother. All manner of craftwork, produce, and fancy work will be on sale, and gifts to stock the shop will be gratefully received.

Arrangements were made to collect donations sent by country people, such as eggs, butter, dressed poultry, jams etc., from Flinders Street or Spencer Street stations twice a day. There was an excellent response to this request, and the League decided to sell all the unsold goods by auction at 6 pm on the last day of opening. Mrs Lort Smith reported to the *Herald* that the shop had also been used to explain the work of the League to members of the public, and many donations had been received.

Mrs O. Gibson of Toorak had prepared a craftwork display valued at about £60. She was to continue to make intricate craftwork for the League until at least the outbreak of the war.

Mrs Oswald Gibson with her dolls' house
Tintern Hall, *AWL scrapbook.*

Mrs Oswald Gibson's Centenary Market,
The Sun, 14 August 1934, *AWL scrapbook.*

It was reported in the press in 1933 that Lady Lyle, who had been selling flowers and fruit from her garden for nearly twenty years to assist philanthropic funds, was giving the proceeds from the sales to the Animal Welfare Hospital at Parkville for the sick animals of the poor. 'Her Japanese cherry blossom, which is very beautiful and very decorative, is now available, and lilies of the valley will be ready in a week.'

Other events held in 1933 included a ball at the Rex Ballroom on 31 October, and Miss Marion Montgomery's annual dance for young people at the St Kilda Town Hall on Saturday 29 October.

The ball at the Rex was attended by the Governor-General with Lady Isaacs

wearing a black velvet wrap with a collar of white fox over her ivory white gown with its crystal embroidery. A lovely bouquet of roses and lily of the valley was presented to her by the president of the league (Mrs Norman Brookes), whose gown of faint corn-coloured satin had wide cape sleeves edged with beige fur ... Hawaiian garlands of white watsonia blossoms (made by Mrs Brookes and her daughters) were worn by each member of the committee, and, together with gay balloons, were also sold in aid of the funds.

Another feature of the ball was a special skipping dance, performed by Miss Maisie Cowper and accompanied by Messrs Alaric Howitt and Fred Dennett. Members of the Gilbert and Sullivan Opera Company and Miss Dorothy Peters, leading lady in 'Autumn Crocus', had promised to attend after the theatres had closed.

Marion Montgomery's ball was described in some detail by the *Herald* on the following day. The hall was decorated in tones of sunny yellow and pale blossom pink:

> *Canopies of blossoms swayed over the heads of the dancers, and quaint pink and gold lanterns crossbarred with dark bands cast a radiant light over silken frocks and velvet capes. Miss Montgomery received her guests wearing a gown of black romaine with a cluster of diamente blossoms fastened at the shoulder. Her brocade cloak was in blended colouring with a collar of soft dark fur. Mrs U. J. Nicholas (who is on the committee of the Animal Welfare League) wore a black georgette gown with a sash of petal pink and brown peau d'ange ribbon.*

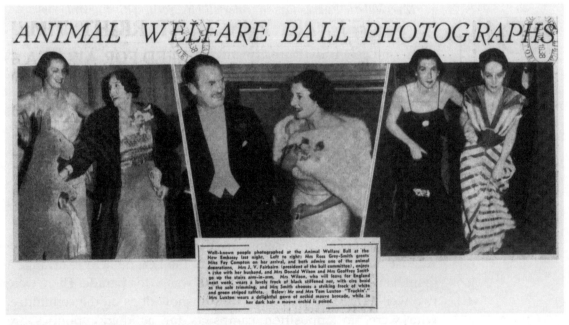

People attending the Animal Welfare League Ball, *Herald,* **29 July 1938,**
Newspaper Collection, State Library of Victoria.

Some of the bright and beautiful revellers were described:

Many Beauties at the Welfare Ball

Our sympathies were all with anyone who could not gain admittance to the Animal Welfare Ball at the Rex, because it was a very good dance.

Edna Kirby danced several little numbers, but was at her best in a pert little polka ... the local beauties and their country cousins present looked extremely attractive. Miss Marjorie Stephens was among the most distinctive of the young people, in scarlet and parakeet green. The little fitted jacket was of scarlet organdie, with pierrot frills about the shoulders, and the frock was of green crepe with a scarlet band about the hem.

Miss Patricia Mills was fair and tall in a black and white chiffon with fine plaid stripes.

Deep crimson roses gave the only colour to Mrs Rupert Fanning's white crepe sokol. Titian-haired Miss Betty Matear's frockings were grape blue with blue ostrich feathers curling about the shoulders.

Quaker grey crepe was chosen by Miss Mary Baillieu who heightened the illusion with a three tiered cape about the shoulders.

Miss Valerie Purves was in waterfall blue satin with a narrow ribbon tied about her hair.

Later in 1933 Lady Fairbairn and her husband, Sir George, opened their home at 'Greenlay', Mount Martha, for a fete. The *Herald* reported on 11 November 1933:

Members of the Savages Club will grill, for public consumption, $1\frac{1}{2}$ cwt (hundredweight) of chops in the open air and Sydney will furnish 140 dozen of her choicest oysters. Sir George himself will preside over a guessing competition, touching the weight of one of his black-faced sheep.

Miss Marjorie Millear organised a golf day to raise funds on 19 April 1934. Mrs Lort Smith and Marion Montgomery set up a provisions stall.

But it was not all plain sailing in the fundraising field. *The Leader* (8 August 1934) reported on a meeting of the League held to arrange a gymkhana. One of the items suggested was a dog parade. There were two well-known factions of owners of show dogs on the committee, who were 'in opposition camps as far as doggy politics are

concerned'. The committee was split between the two factions, but regardless of this a committee was formed of all those who wished to work together in a good cause. However, it was realised that this would not be acceptable because all those who were subject to the conditions imposed by the Kennel Control Council would be suspended if they were on the committee with anyone connected with the opposition, so they had to resign from the new committee.

Despite this the gymkhana was a success. It was held on a perfect sunny day. Amongst the dignitaries who attended were the president of the occasion and his wife, Sir Robert and Lady Knox, and the League Patroness, Lady Huntingfield. As well as riding events there were a variety of stalls, a whippet race, a fancy dress parade of dogs and a display by the mounted police.

Barbecue given by Sir George and Lady Fairbairn, AWL scrapbook.

Ticket Secretaries for the Animal Welfare League Ball, *Herald*, 3 July 1937, *AWL scrapbook*.

Another highly successful ball was held in 1938, described in the 'Melbourne Letters' of Sydney's *Sun and Guardian* as the week's most important social event. 'Everything was merry as a marriage bell with lovely women in magnificent frocks all trying to look as beautiful as Mrs J. V. Fairbairn, Peggy Foster that was.' Mrs Fairbairn was the president of the ball committee. The article continued:

> No one has ever been able to resist Lady Lyle and Mrs Lort Smith who jointly founded the Animal Welfare hospital where poor people's pets are treated free of charge. They give their time and money. And they have built the loveliest little hospital way up in North Melbourne, which must seem to the doggies and cats, to say nothing of other fauna brought there, a real animal paradise.

A variety of fundraising functions including bridge parties, raffles and tin rattling at social events continued to be held until the outbreak of war, when fetes became the League's major source of fundraising.

Fundraising in the City, *Sun*, 27
September 1935, *AWL scrapbook*.

Rallying to the cause – committee for
a bridge party meets at the home of
Mrs Nelken (extreme left), 1939,
AWL scrapbook.

A group of committee members for the annual bridge party and market fair to
be held at 9 Darling street on July 25 in aid of the Animal Welfare League,
photographed in the garden of Mrs. Louis Nelken's (extreme left) home.

War years: 1939-1945

Some idea of the stress caused by war can be gauged from the opening remarks made by the League president, Lady (formerly Mrs) Brookes, at the opening of the annual general meeting on 14 May 1942:

> *In these times we were all of us divided in our minds and very occupied in our thoughts, and it was very difficult, speaking for the Committee, to concentrate on one special thing.*

But there were other more personal stresses which influenced the running of the hospital.

Mrs Lort Smith's sister, Miss Montgomery, died a year after the outbreak of the war, on 1 September 1940. Mrs Lort Smith was granted leave for three weeks from 13 September, but on 8 October she told a meeting of the Board that she intended to resign immediately. Both Mrs Halley and Lady Lyle asked Mrs Lort Smith to reconsider her decision, and asked Lady Brookes to talk with her. After a telephone discussion between the two women Mrs Lort Smith agreed to suspend her resignation for one month.

It seems likely, from subsequent events, that Mrs Lort Smith's resignation was related to the decision to draw up a constitution for the hospital which would remove her position of directress. In 1932 the League had discussed becoming

Miss Marion Montgomery,
The Animal Lover book of the Animal Welfare League, **1940.**

incorporated but the decision was that 'the work of the League would be hampered by losing much elasticity in the management of its undertakings', and the matter did not proceed. This meant that the hospital had been run without a constitution. At the October meeting, when Mrs Lort Smith expressed her intention to resign, the Board agreed with its legal adviser, Mr Weigall, that they should become incorporated and that he should draw up a constitution to make the League a legal entity and remove personal responsibility from individual members.

It was recorded at the November meeting that 'the President invited Mrs Lort Smith to return to the Hospital and work as before until the constitution was drawn up. Mrs Lort Smith applied for a further two months leave of absence'. The meeting granted a one-month extension.

Mrs Nelken, *The Animal Lover book of the Animal Welfare League,* **1940.**

The draft constitution was presented to the Executive Committee by Mr Weigall on 1 December 1940 and was ratified at a meeting on 14 January 1941. Lady Brookes then directed that a letter be sent to Mrs Lort Smith saying that the general committee hoped she would become a member of the house committee of three, the other two members being Lady Brookes and Mrs Halley. This committee would meet weekly to discuss hospital matters. A second letter was sent on 18 February 1941 asking her to be at the hospital the following week if she wished to serve on the house committee but she sent her apologies to the next meeting with a refusal to join the committee.

An application for incorporation was made on 5 May 1941, the date of the annual general meeting, under the names of:

Ruby Dugan	Wife of the Governor of Victoria
Mabel Balcombe Brookes	Married Woman
Isabel Clare Lyle	Married Woman
Louisa Eleanor Lort Smith	Widow
Lorna Bessie Fairbairn	Domestic Duties

A licence was issued on 30 June 1941 registering the Animal Welfare League of Victoria as a company with limited liability under the provisions of the *Companies Act 1938.*

The articles of association listed Lady Dugan as patroness, Lady Brookes as president, and Lady Fairbairn and Mrs Louis Nelken both as vice-presidents. Fifteen other members were named including Mrs Lort Smith.

Mrs Lort Smith attended the annual general meeting of the Animal Welfare League on 5 May 1941 and Lady Brookes welcomed her back after her long absence. In July 1941 she asked, through Lady Brookes, for permission to open an account in the State Savings Bank in Toorak for a special collection of funds. But she did not attend any Executive committee meetings or send apologies until she attended a meeting on 24 March 1942. Why did she return at that time? Perhaps it was because by then the hospital was in crisis and she recognised that her management skills were needed.

Ron Greville was not called up until almost twelve months after the war had started. The question of whether or not he should be paid whilst attending military camp had come up for discussion in October 1939 but no immediate decision was made. On 28 November 1939 it was agreed that he should meet with Mrs Lort Smith and Mrs Nelken to discuss drawing up a new contract, so evidently their decision not to give him a second year had either been overlooked or overturned. Mr Weigall, their honorary solicitor, was then asked to draw up a contract which 'includes the condition that further Camp Leave should not be paid for beyond the ordinary fourteen days, a further condition that need for the Surgeon's services on active service automatically breaks the contract'. It was also to be written into the contract that the League was required to give one month's notice of termination of contract, while Mr Greville was required to give three months' notice, a clause which was deleted on the advice of Mr Weigall after Mr Greville objected.

Mr Greville was called up and resigned on 28 August 1941. His resignation was received by the Board with regret but when he requested that the Board pay him two weeks' salary on account of leave, because he had worked for eight months, they only did so on the recommendation of Mr Weigall who gave his call-up as a reason for a show of generosity.

Ron Greville was influenced by the calibre of the medical men he had met during his period of service, particularly his term of imprisonment by the Japanese. On his return from the war he decided to study medicine, which he could do as part of his rehabilitation as a returned serviceman. He also returned to the hospital for a short time as a locum, and operated a night service, but his services were terminated in September 1947 with the appointment of a permanent vet, Mr McNelis. After graduating in medicine Ron worked in research at the Commonwealth Serum Laboratories. He had four children and eleven grandchildren. His wife Nan died in Canberra in 2000, and Ron died about six months later in 2001.

Nan Greville received two personal letters from Lady Lyle which she showed to Gerry Clarkson. They are quoted in full, with her consent, because they tell us a good deal about the personality of Lady Lyle and the stress everyone suffered during the war years. The first letter was dated May 30. No year was given, but the context suggests that it would have been 1940, when Ron was working at the hospital and before he left for the war. Both had the address 225 Walsh Street, South Yarra.

My dear Mrs Greville,

Will you forgive me for not having written to you before – I have thought much about you and often – Congratulations on the arrival of the dear babe – and I trust father has not to walk too much floor at nights – of course I hear of you from time to time. It is very difficult to get a word with your husband on Mon or Fri – he may not have noticed but most days I pop into his room but retire quickly when I see four legs in the air or a wide open mouth! But seriously – I am thinking of you & indeed of us all – times are harder than some of us can bear, but you are young & you have the boy and someone to share your sorrows & joy & I know you will be brave & stand up to it. My daughter Dr Mary Herring has her husband away & is looking forward to the happy day of his return – How splendid of our men – and you would not have it otherwise I feel sure.

What we shall do I dare not think but these matters sink into insignificance when the big things come along.

Please accept sympathy and encouragement.
Yours sincerely
Clare Lyle

The second letter was undated. Ron had served in a medical unit but had been taken prisoner by the Japanese, and was sent to work on the Burma railway.

Dear Mrs Greville

I only heard your good news today & I must write & tell you how glad I am for you. – So many people have hearts almost breaking with suspense & it is very terrible. – I wonder how long you will have to wait before his arms will be round you – that will be the real thing – but still we are grateful for good news.

I am just out of Hos(pital) after 6 weeks or more on my back after removal of cataract on eyes & still feel shaky.

The eye business was simple & well done & I should have been back in 2 wks – but as a matter of fact I had no heart to return here to an empty house – it is all too sad & since my light went out nothing seems worthwhile.

How splendid that Mr Greville is fit & well but even so life will never be quite the same. One cannot fight these things.

Yrs very sinc.
Clare Lyle.

Sir Thomas Lyle, Clare's husband, had died in 1944 and she is almost certainly referring to his death when she says 'since my light went out'.

Finding a vet to replace Ron Greville was not an easy task. In July 1939, shortly before the outbreak of war, a new agency had been set up to regulate employment. It was necessary that any person recommended for appointment to a professional position be cleared by the Director of Manpower to ensure that the appointee was not needed for war work. Thus past difficulties in obtaining veterinary staff were exacerbated by this additional bureaucratic requirement, and the fact that most young and able-bodied people were already working for the war effort.

Mr McManamny was appointed as full-time locum vet for one month and then his position was extended, on a part-time basis, for three half-days a week. The assistant, Simon Fraser, who by now had four years' hospital experience, was called on to make up for the loss of a full-time vet, and he was given an honorarium in compensation.

LADY LYLE returning a four-footed patient to its anxious owners at the Royal Park Veterinary Clinic yesterday. She plays a leading part in the activities of the institution.

In December 1940 the Board discussed two applications for veterinary surgeon. Mrs Nelken proposed that Mr Butler be appointed at £500 per annum, but Lady Lyle wanted to appoint Mr Barraclough, who was demanding £700. Lady Lyle demonstrated her support for her candidate by offering to make up the difference of £200 if Mr Barraclough was appointed, and this was agreed to. He made a very positive impression on the Board, and at the annual general meeting held in 1941 Lady Brookes was to make a special reference to his very fine work – he had 'more than justified his appointment'.

Mr Barraclough's contract was renewed for a further twelve months on 10 February 1942. Almost a month later he asked to work part-time, from 1.30 pm to 6 pm instead of 9 am to 6 pm, for the salary of £450 per annum. He told the Board that he felt sure that he would be able to cover his workload within this shorter period of time. The Board, as so often happened, decided to hold over making a decision until the matter had been discussed with Lady Brookes. After considerable discussion the Board finally decided to reduce the hospital hours in line with Mr Barraclough's suggestion. Unfortunately the result was a disastrous financial loss, and it seems that the Board used Mr Barraclough as the scapegoat – after all, the original suggestion of shorter hospital hours had come from him.

The huge loss of clients and earnings threatened the viability of the hospital. It was so serious that the Board had to consider whether the hospital could continue to operate. It decided that it should continue full-time operation for the present, but that a house sub-committee meeting should be held to discuss future strategies. Lady Brookes announced that 'the time for sentiment was passed, and the pruning knife must be used'. The sub-committee of Mrs Lort Smith, Mrs Nelken, Mrs Trathan, Mrs Halley and Miss Norwood met on the two succeeding days, together with a representative of Mr Treloar, the honorary treasurer, who pointed out that, while the hospital had operated very successfully during 1940 and 1941, in the latter year the working deficit of £869 had been turned into a surplus of £508. However, the months of March and April 1942 were the worst in the history of the hospital.

> Mr Treloar was one of the founder members of the League and was for many years its honorary treasurer. He was one of the four men who volunteered to form the finance advisory committee in 1955, in which year he was elected to the Board. He resigned on 30 June 1961. Dame Mabel Brookes spoke warmly of the services Mr Treloar had rendered to the League from the date of its inception and expressed the Board's great regret of that he had decided to resign his office. Mr Treloar had two sisters on the Board, Mrs Perry and Miss Daisy Treloar.

Although Mr Barraclough indicated his willingness to continue to work for the League his contract was not renewed when it expired at the end of June. He subsequently enrolled in a course to study medicine. The sub-committee recommended that a woman be appointed as veterinary surgeon, possibly because women were paid less than men. Was it a coincidence that an application from Miss Farr had already been received by the Board in the previous month? She was later appointed on a salary of £450 – substantially below Mr Barraclough's salary of £700.

On 12 May 1942 Lady Brookes told the annual general meeting that Mr Barraclough would be leaving in about six weeks and continued:

They were fortunate in having had the services of Mr Barraclough who was a very good surgeon indeed, and who had been very kind and done everything he could for the Hospital. She wished to place on record an appreciation of his splendid work while at the Hospital.

Since it was Lady Brookes herself who had refused to renew his contract, this either was hypocritical or, if she firmly believed her statement, reinforces the point that his dismissal had more to do with saving money than with quality of professional service.

The sub-committee which had recommended Mr Barraclough's dismissal also recommended that the staff should be told that the Executive was making every effort to keep the hospital open, and be asked for their fullest cooperation. They were also to be consulted regularly for their ideas and suggestions, and to have closer contact with the Executive committee. It is notable throughout the history of the League that invariably in times of stress a similar recommendation has been made. Unfortunately, once things started to get back on an even keel this recommendation was almost always forgotten.

Ann Flashman treating an Alsatian, 1942, *The Sun*, 18 June 1942, *AWL scrapbook*.

Mrs Cyril Trathan, *Animal Lover book of the Animal Welfare League*, 1940.

Mrs Cyril Trathan was the wife of a senior executive of the Melbourne Metropolitan Board of Works. She was a founder member of the League and a vice-president, a position which she took very seriously. She was very interested in cat protection. She was remembered as a stern woman who was strict with the staff. She was described by Phyl Taylor as a bit 'school marmish' and indeed she proposed many of the more conservative decisions made by the Board. She was particularly concerned that the staff should maintain a high standard of dress and deportment, and she was opposed to staff having long hair and wearing jewellery. In February 1954 the motion was passed on her proposition that 'Councillors must stand when addressing the Chair'. She resigned from the Board in 1976 and died in the same year.

Ann Flashman, who had been the first full-time veterinary surgeon to be employed at the Lost Dogs' Home, worked temporarily for the hospital while a new appointment was being made. She was employed for five half-days a week at a salary of £10.

Kathleen Farr was given a two-year contract in June 1942. She had graduated from the University of Sydney in 1938 and had worked for the New South Wales Department of Agriculture. She was described by the *Herald* (25 June 1942) as bringing 'youth and enthusiasm' to her new job, as well as an interest in human psychology:

Dogs reflect their owner's personality just as children reflect their parents' according to Miss Kathleen Farr.

In treating an animal Miss Farr always tries to ascertain the make-up of the owner. She thus brings to her work a knowledge and understanding of human beings as well as animals.

The hospital took the opportunity of the appointment of a new vet to re-examine its policy of neutering animals. The matter was previously discussed in April 1941 and it had been agreed to leave decisions to the discretion of the vet and the house committee, but in August 1942 the Board decided that animals would not be spayed at the hospital. Since no arguments were recorded for or against this decision it is hard to ascertain the basis for the policy – the only consistent factor was that it never stayed the same for long. It was not until 1988 that a firm policy was defined.

There is no record of Lady Lyle's reaction to the sacking of Mr Barraclough, but there is evidence that she did not approve of the work of his replacement Kathleen Farr, and it seems that it was disagreement with members of the Board about various connected issues, some of which related to Miss Farr's treatment of her patients, which led to Lady Lyle's very public resignation from the Board and the subsequent removal of her name from the title of the hospital.

At a meeting on 12 October 1942 the Board received a letter of resignation from Lady Lyle. No reason was recorded for her resignation, and the Board accepted it, 'with regret'. Lady Brookes said she would write to Lady Lyle, and a letter signed by the honorary secretary was sent to Lady Lyle which read:

Your letter of September 20th was received with regret at a meeting of the Council held at the hospital on October 12th.

The members feel deeply your wish to sever your connection with the activities of the League, and will miss your valuable help at all times so willingly given.

Following her resignation, Lady Lyle wrote to various newspapers saying that she was no longer involved with the Animal Welfare League. *The Argus* published a single paragraph on 14 November 1942:

Lady Lyle and the A.W.L. Hospital

Lady Lyle who has for many years taken an active interest in animal welfare, desires it to be known that she has resigned her membership of the committee of the Animal Welfare League Hospital.

On 17 November 1942 one of the members of the committee, Mrs Keep, told a meeting that Lady Lyle had sought and obtained permission from Lady Brookes to write to the press, but Lady Brookes denied this. The minutes then record:

In view of Lady Lyle's letter to the press ... and her statement to other people, the Committee feel that they do not wish to have any further communication with Lady Lyle, nor that any of the dogs from her home be accommodated in this Hospital.

The staff to be told not to discuss the affairs of the League with any person not a member of the Council.

Although Lady Lyle appears to have written to several if not all the newspapers, the only one to publish an account of the dispute between the Board and Lady Lyle was *Truth*. On 21 November 1942 she is reported to have said her resignation was the result of having been handed out the greatest insult the committee could have offered her. She complained that some dreadful things had been going on in the inpatient section, but that when she had put her list of complaints to a Board meeting Miss Farr had been called in to give an explanation but had contradicted Lady Lyle, asserting that the patients were doing very well, which Lady Lyle knew to be untrue.

Another contentious issue was the right of Board members to have free access to the surgeries, which questioned the surgeon's right to professional autonomy. The matter had indeed been discussed at a Board meeting on 8 September 1942:

Mrs Lort Smith supported Mrs Trathan's suggestion that no member of the Committee should go into the Inpatient's Department before first asking the permission of the Surgeon, and Lady Brookes, in moving an amendment, said 'Do not give away your rights as Committee members to visit any part of the hospital at any time but for expediency and courtesy it is advisable to notify the veterinary surgeon.'

Lady Lyle later told *Truth* that there had been an embargo on members of the committee entering the in-patient section without permission from the veterinary surgeon. This was publicly denied by Lady Brookes, who also publicly supported the work of Miss Farr, and refuted some specific allegations which Lady Lyle had made. This included Lady Lyle's assertion that two dogs that should have been destroyed were treated by Miss Farr, with Lady Brookes maintaining that the vets' work was to cure animals not to destroy them. 'Sometimes, to achieve a cure, the animal has to suffer some pain. It is the same with human beings.' The League had sought advice from a leading veterinary surgeon who had said that 'he could do no more for the dogs than what was being done'.

At a special meeting held on 26 November a letter from the editor of the *Herald* to Mrs Lort Smith was read. It related to Lady Lyle's letter to the press. Unfortunately the contents were not recorded, but it drew the response from Mrs Nelken that 'Lady Lyle should be answered in like manner'. After general discussion it was agreed that no such action be taken. It was then moved that

> the name Lyle be removed from the Hospital Building, Ambulance, and Stationery, in accordance with Lady Lyle's wish and Mr Weigall's ruling.

There is nothing like secrecy to breed rumour and speculation, and the edict of the Board certainly helped to foster much conjecture. The *Truth* article was not amongst the other newspaper cuttings held in hospital scrapbooks, and has only recently come to light.

It is evident from her letters to the press over some time that Lady Lyle continued to lobby for reforms to the provision of animal welfare, and in 1947 she attended the annual general meeting and was re-elected to the League's Executive on the proposal of Mrs Lort Smith. Unfortunately ill health prevented her from attending any subsequent meetings. She died in May 1949.

A new pharmacist, Miss Neilsen, had also commenced work with Kathleen Farr in June 1942. On 9 March 1943 she wrote to Lady Brookes enclosing a copy of the Dispensaries Board Award which showed that as a Chief Pharmaceutical Chemist she should be paid £8 10s 6d per week. She said that 'owing to the tremendous increases in

Miss Kathleen Farr, new veterinary surgeon, observing Miss L. Neilsen at work in her pharmacy, *The Argus*, 23 June 1942, *Newspaper Collection, State Library of Victoria.*

the cost of living and the high rate of income tax, I find it impossible to continue at the present wage of £5 per week'. She verbally told the Board that she would accept £7 10s a week and this was agreed to.

Kathleen Farr enlisted in the army a few months after Lady Lyle's resignation. A special meeting of the Animal Welfare League was held on 30 March 1943 to discuss how she was to be replaced and this meeting was also attended by Mr Jones, president of the Australian Veterinary Association, who told the Board that 'he would be pleased to afford the Animal Welfare League any assistance he could to replace Miss Farr'. In the interim Mr McManamny agreed to continue as a relieving vet for one-and-a-half hours daily until a replacement could be found.

Another prominent member of the AVA at this time was its vice-president and immediate past president, Dr Heslop. He was well known to the League through his appointment as Director of Animal First Aid which was set up under the Federal Air Raid Precautions program. He had also spoken at the League's most recent annual general meeting. He was invited to become a member of the Animal Welfare League Committee as a representative of the AVA, an offer which he accepted.

Dr G. G. Heslop graduated from Melbourne Veterinary School in 1913. Shortly after graduation he fought in the First World War where he was awarded the DSO. On his return to Melbourne he gained his doctorate in veterinary science in 1921, and joined the staff of the University of Melbourne. He became a fellow of the Walter and Eliza Hall Institute for his work on the diagnosis of pleuropneumonia in cattle.

Dr Heslop had seen the effects of war and worked with wounded horses during his war service in France so at the outbreak of the Second World War he was well qualified to lead the Air Raid Precautions for animals in Victoria. He also held the position of official veterinarian to the Victoria Racing Club, although his duties during the war years were not onerous, allowing him to became involved with the Animal Welfare League. He retained an association with the hospital until at least the end of the 1940s.

On 4 June 1943 both Dr Heslop and Mr Jones (AVA) attended a meeting of the hospital committee. They reported that it had not been possible to find a replacement vet – there was simply no one available. They then offered to approach the Lost Dogs' Home with a view to sharing its vet, but Mr Jones immediately backtracked and said he could not approach them until the League made certain economies, particularly relating to the pharmacy and ambulance service, to bring them into line with the Lost Dogs' Home. It was also necessary for the League to adopt the same scale of charges as the Home. Mr Jones also advised that it was uneconomical for the hospital to employ a pharmacist as he had been told by the locum vet Mr McManamny that every bottle of medicine was costing the League thirty shillings (equivalent to about $3 at that time) in labour, and that all prescriptions could be prepared in one day during the week, and vaccines could be obtained from the Commonwealth Serum Laboratories as required.

Dr Heslop pointed out that the AVA could not continue indefinitely to disregard the fact that an assistant, Simon Fraser, was doing the work of a trained vet, and he made the suggestion that two representatives from the AVA meet with two delegates from the Lost Dogs' Home and the League for further discussion. This was agreed to and a further meeting time arranged for the following week.

This meeting did not take place, however, as one of the Lost Dogs' Home representatives was unable to attend, and Mr Jones was also unavailable. Dr Heslop reported to the next meeting of the League that Mr Jones had 'told him quite definitely that he would not take part in the conference until certain economies, as suggested by himself, had been made in the management of the hospital'. He had asked Dr Heslop to convey to the Board the points on which he insisted, but Dr Heslop had refused to do so and advised Mr Jones to meet the Board and state his views himself.

Dr Heslop put his own point of view to the meeting-that the overhead costs were very high, but he did not think it advisable to reduce expenses at the cost of efficiency. He then offered to take on a locum position with the League from 9.45 am until 12 noon daily, on the same basis as Mr McManamny, who had not been able to continue as a locum. However, he insisted that he have one day off every month, and that the arrangement could only be temporary until such time as the Victoria Racing Club required his services full-time.

A special meeting of the Board was held on 19 July 1943, attended by Dr Heslop and Mr Weigall, the League's honorary legal adviser. Dr Heslop told Mr Weigall that his appointment to the Executive Committee was to help the League through a difficult time but that 'his association had imposed on him more than he was prepared to do' – presumably to bring about the changes which Mr Jones thought necessary. Mr Weigall replied that he

> could not understand the attitude taken up by the Veterinary Association inasmuch as they were unable to help the League by obtaining the services of a surgeon, nor was the hospital serviced by Honorary Surgeons. Since private Veterinary Surgeons are so overworked he failed to see where the A.W.L. was encroaching and he considered it a piece of impertinence for the Veterinary Association to interfere with the domestic arrangements of the A.W.L. provided that it was such as to give proper service to the animals.

Mr Brettingham-Moore,
Herald, **30 June 1945,** *Lost Dogs' Home scrapbook.*

In August Dr Heslop reported to the Board that he had tried to ascertain from the AVA just what further concessions were required of the League, but was unable to get any very definite information. All reasonable demands had been met. These included obtaining signatures on the record cards and history sheets, and a change to the wording on the outside wall. He had understood that once these concessions were made the AVA would be satisfied.

In July 1943 the League received an application from Mr Brettingham-Moore who was currently employed in Brisbane in a teaching and research capacity. Before his appointment could be made it had to be agreed by the Scientific Manpower (Veterinary) Advisory Committee.

Mr Brettingham-Moore also wrote to the AVA requesting information about the work of the League. He received a reply almost immediately – a telegram stating 'Position very unsatisfactory. Writing. Gorrie'. The letter which followed, dated 20 July 1943 and signed by Mr Gorrie, honorary secretary of the Victorian Division of the AVA, made several points. The first was concerned with the relationship between the League and the AVA:

We have been more or less intimately associated with this charitable organisation for about ten years. We have endeavoured to co-operate with the League authorities because we feel that there is a definite place in the community for a Veterinary hospital to treat the sick animals of poor people. Co-operation by the League's Committee has fluctuated markedly- rising to a maximum whenever there was difficulty in obtaining an efficient veterinary surgeon for the Hospital, but rapidly receding to a minimum when such difficulties were overcome.

The second point concerned the relationship between the League and the four vets it had employed. The letter stated that the relationship between the League and its veterinarians was apparently congenial during the first few months, but invariably differences arose which finally developed into 'more or less open hostility'.

The third point questioned the treatment of animals belonging to persons well able to pay veterinary fees:

The Committee of the League has always stated its willingness to restrict treatment to sick animals of poor people, but we have had so many authenticated cases in which this policy was not adhered to that latterly we have come to the conclusion that their undertaking in the matter is valueless.

The fourth point was that there was insufficient work for a full-time vet. The letter alleged that the work of the League had fallen off considerably since 1939. It continued that Elizabeth Harvey, a vet currently employed by the Lost Dogs' Home, was not fully occupied and that the two organisations would be better off sharing her services. The AVA was therefore recommending to the Scientific Manpower (Veterinary) Advisory Committee that no vet be allowed to take up the appointment.

The letter also discussed the relationship between the Board and Dr Heslop. Mr Gorrie maintained that when Dr Heslop had accepted a position on the Board of the League he had intended to foster the amalgamation between the League and the SPCA but:

We have now fairly strong evidence to indicate that important matters of policy which should have been referred to Dr Heslop were decided without his knowledge. Dr Heslop has, therefore, decided to bring matters to a head at the next Committee Meeting of the League, and it is possible that this might result in a final severance of relations between this Division and the League.

Mr Brettingham-Moore sent a copy of this letter to Dr Heslop, who in turn showed it to the Board. They proposed that Mr Weigall be asked to write to the AVA for an explanation. Since the League could not afford to further antagonise the AVA it was finally agreed that the matter be left in abeyance until a definite decision was reached about the appointment of a permanent veterinary surgeon.

Dr Heslop was outraged at the actions of the AVA and he confronted Mr Gorrie and Dr Jones. Probably as a result of Dr Heslop's criticism and the threat of possible legal action Mr Gorrie wrote a further letter to Mr Brettingham-Moore dated 21 August and toning down the accusations against the League:

On re-perusal of the letter, we think that that statement endeavours too baldly to express our views and that it may possibly be liable to misconstruction. We therefore desire to make known to you that we did not mean to impute any want of good faith in the Committee of the League, since we did not, and do not doubt that the undertaking, when given, was intended to be carried out. We realised, however, that probably owing to the difficulty of ascertaining who are poor persons it cannot be given effect to in most cases – hence our opinion that the undertaking would not help matters. It is of course common knowledge that there are many people who will untruthfully plead poverty to save expense in any direction.

Dr Heslop resigned from the AVA, although he was later persuaded by colleagues to resign only from his position as vice-president. He also wrote a personal letter to Mr Brettingham-Moore saying that, as the AVA representative on the Board, he considered that he should have been shown a draft of the letter before it was sent, and that several statements in it were not true 'apart from the fact that some of them might even be regarded as malicious'. He continued:

Since taking up the position the attitude of the members of the A.W.L. Committee towards me personally and through me to the A.V.A. has been most cordial and friendly, and I have not had the slightest difficulty in having any suggestion of mine carried out promptly. As a matter of fact the A.W.L. Committee gave me carte blanche to institute any reforms which I considered to be necessary. The position, therefore, was that the A.V.A. had me – their vice president – representing them on the A.W.L. committee and in virtual control of the affairs of the A.W.L.; a situation which is without precedent. (Letter 17 August 1943)

Dr Heslop and the League were very keen to appoint Mr Brettingham-Moore, but there were delays attributed to the Manpower Board. Dr Brettingham-Moore, at age forty-nine and with four young children, would not have been considered for active service. He was employed at the Animal Health Station run by the Queensland Department of Agriculture. When, after much argument, this department finally agreed to release him, the Scientific Advisory Committee of Manpower put up an objection on the basis of the 'uneconomical animal thesis'. In other words, there was no economic value in looking after pets. Dr Heslop was still in charge of the Air Raid Precautions (ARP) program, and was therefore responsible for looking after the horses at the Queen Victoria Market. He used this argument to enlist the support of Dr Clunies Ross who was attached to the veterinary school at the University of Sydney and who dealt with the management of the ARP program. He was dismayed to learn from Dr Clunies Ross's reply that the program was to be curtailed in the southern states and he was not able to support the appointment.

The League and Mr Brettingham-Moore then decided on a new tactic. He applied for a position with the Victorian Department of Agriculture stating he was available to work every afternoon, which would give him the freedom to work for the League every morning. Although the Victorian Department refused his application for part-time work, the Manpower Board did finally agree to his taking up his job with the League. The decision seems to have been influenced by the intervention of Mrs Lort Smith's former dancing student, Harold Holt. He was then a federal member of parliament, and he accompanied a deputation of Mrs Lort Smith, Mrs Nelken and Lady Brookes to a meeting to lobby for Mr Brettingham-Moore's appointment. An undated letter addressed to Mrs Lort Smith from the Federal Member Rooms, Melbourne, said 'Let's hope our joint efforts will prove successful. With kind regards, sincerely Harold Holt'.

They were successful. Mr Brettingham-Moore finally took up the position in January 1945. He remained with the League for only one year, leaving early in 1946 to return to his home state of Tasmania. He gave no reason for his resignation, and it was evident that the committee respected his period of service because in 1949 when they were finding it difficult to recruit staff they wrote to ask him if he would return.

By the 1940s the fortunes of the Victorian Society for the Protection of Animals, also referred to as the SPCA had improved and in 1943 it had over 50,000 members. In November 1941 the VSPA approached the League about possible amalgamation. It was agreed that the matter be 'treated informally for the time being', and Lady Brookes said that she would discuss the matter with Mr A. L. Keep, honorary secretary of the VSPA. On 12 October 1942 Mrs Lort Smith was asked at a Board meeting to write to the secretary of the VSPA to ask their views about amalgamation, and in December Lady Brookes again recommended the amalgamation should take place as soon as possible.

Dr Heslop wrote to Mr Keep in July 1943 regarding amalgamation. Mr Keep replied saying that the committee of the VSPA had carefully considered the question, but that a letter from Mr Jones written on 20 July 1943, stating that there was a serious divergence of opinion between the AWL and the AVA, had influenced them to turn down the proposition:

> Since the V.S.P.A. enjoys the happiest relations with both the Animal Welfare League and the Australian Veterinary Association, the Committee of this Society resolve that in view of the unfortunate difference which appears to exist between the A.W.L. and the A.V.A. the moment is not an opportune one for considering proposals for the amalgamation of the A.W.L. and the V.S.P.A.

It was the view of Mr Jones (which he included in his letter to Mr Brettingham-Moore) that once amalgamation had taken place

the SPCA would mainly control the League's Hospital, and we feel that the whole matter would then be on a much more satisfactory and ethical basis. The feeling of our members who have been in close contact with the SPCA is that following the hypothetical amalgamation, a representative of this Division would be appointed to the controlling body and his advice would carry much weight in all veterinary matters.

It is clear from this letter that the AVA was keen for the amalgamation between the League and the SPCA to take place so it is ironic that the reason why the SPCA turned down the proposal was the bad feeling between the League and the AVA. It is also ironic that the AVA did not appear to recognise that the outcome which it was working towards – a closer control of the League's affairs – was, according to Mr Heslop, already achieved.

Other problems caused by the war included the need to take precautions against bombing raids, shortages of materials and in particular food and petrol rationing. In June 1941 it was reported that the method of destroying cats needed to be discussed because of the increase in price, and possible rationing, of chloroform.

Air Raid Precautions were first mentioned on 20 January 1942 when Lady Brookes asked for a committee meeting to be called to discuss the formation of an ARP plan for animals. The hospital had been nominated as a first aid post – whether for animals or humans is not clear. A lecture was given by Dr Heslop, who had been put in charge of animal rescue for the duration of the war. The Japanese bombing of Darwin in which 240 people lost their lives took place on 20 February 1942. This would no doubt have added to the impetus to improve the security of the hospital.

There was some correspondence between the League's architect, Leighton Irwin, and the hospital about providing air raid shelters, and he donated £10 toward the work. It was at this time that Mrs Lort Smith returned to the Board and she immediately began negotiations regarding the air raid precautions and the strengthening of the sick animals' room. She had collected £146 in her special fund and £78 of this was used to pay for the required work. At the first meeting Mrs Lort Smith attended after her long break, on 24 March 1942, she suggested a public appeal for more funds to provide air raid shelters, offering to write to the newspapers.

Petrol rationing meant that the hospital had to curtail the use of its ambulance, leading to fewer animals being treated. In December 1941 the petrol scarcity had led to the suggestion that a room be found in the city for its Board meetings. The February meeting was held at the Mutual Store in Flinders Street. It was very close to Flinders Street station, but one wonders how many of the Board would have travelled to the city using public transport. Subsequent meetings reverted to being held at the hospital.

Towards the end of 1943 the government announced its intention to introduce meat rationing. 'Prudence', a columnist with *The Sun*, wrote an article on 14 December 1943 in response to many letters she had received from the general public urging the government to include pets in their allocation of ration cards. Mrs Lort Smith wrote a letter to the same paper on 31 December requesting that the federal government either make provision for pets, or announce that it was not going to do so, at least to resolve the uncertainty. The government made no such provision, and the Animal Welfare League took the initiative to open up two shops to meet the needs of pet owners.

Meat rationing was introduced on 17 January 1944. There was a weekly ration of between one-and-a-half pounds (680 grams) and four pounds (1.875 kilograms) of meat per person, depending on the quality of the meat purchased. Offal, including heads, trotters and hocks, were excluded from rationing.

Mrs Lort Smith wrote to *The Sun*:

> *Many cats and dogs are being cast adrift, no doubt because of food shortages. This means in most instances a lingering death from starvation and the destruction of bird life. I remind the public again that the Animal Welfare League Hospital receives these creatures and tries to find a suitable home for them, or a merciful end. Instead of turning them adrift, turn your thoughts to this institution and phone F4643. L. E. LORT SMITH, Toorak*

The result of meat rationing and perhaps of Mrs Lort Smith's appeal meant that the number of animals taken to the Lort Smith Animal Hospital increased dramatically. According to the *Herald*, 28 January 1944, 470 cats and 150 dogs had been destroyed since 10 January, while for the same period the previous year the numbers had been 150 cats and 40 dogs. The article continued:

The League asks people not to destroy their pets because of meat rationing. It has recipes for dog biscuits which it is willing to give to anyone, and an animal food shop is to open in Malvern on Tuesday.

Ellie Sansom, registrar of the Lort Smith Animal Hospital, told *The Argus* in January 1944 that so many cats were being brought in for destruction that 'she feared that the rat population might increase as a result'.

Organised by Mrs Lort Smith, the shop in Glenferrie Road, Malvern opened on 2 February 1944. Two retired butchers ran it. It was open every day from 8 am till 5 pm and sold hearts, livers, bullock cheeks and rabbits, and planned, if feasible, to sell horseflesh. Since butchers could not sell horseflesh, alternative arrangements had to be put in place, ensuring adequate refrigeration depots. Dog biscuits were also sold, with ten different varieties on offer including liver and tonic biscuits. On the first day of opening more than 100 customers bought meat between 9 am and 11 am, and 1100 pounds (about 500 kilograms) of meat was sold during the day. By May of that year a second shop had been opened in Camberwell, and between them they sold an average of 3000 to 4000 pounds (about 1360-1800 kilograms) of meat each week. People came from as far away as Dandenong and Frankston to buy meat for their pets.

The first customers at the Animal Welfare League shop in Malvern, *Unidentified newspaper, AWL scrapbook.*

THE CUPBOARD WAS NEARLY BARE when Darkie went to it yesterday at the Animal Welfare League's Hospital in North Melbourne. The institution is one of the hardest hit in the present shortage of fresh meat. The dogs were formerly fed upon uncouponed mutton flaps, but in the present shortage coupons are being demanded and the hospital has no coupon issue.

Later the meat problem became severe. The hospital, with no coupon allocation, was particularly hard hit by a shortage of fresh meat, particularly when coupons were introduced for mutton flaps which had previously been exempt. On 15 March 1946 a photograph in *The Argus* shows a dog at the Lort Smith Animal Hospital staring into an almost empty cupboard. The following day it reported that many gifts had been donated to the hospital as a result of the article.

At the start of the war the hospital was beginning to consolidate its financial position, but as it continued the financial position began to deteriorate. Mr Treloar's report at the first annual general meeting in 1941 stated that the hospital receipts for the last year had been higher than for the previous three years, and that each year the deficiency was being reduced. The League was also receiving substantial support from outside sources by way of legacies and donations. He continued: '... if we can hope to receive more in future there is no reason why the League cannot continue to function'. The League's accounting method was fairly basic, so it was not easy to tell at a glance what money was from a bequest or donation and what was hospital revenue. This was a concern to the honorary treasurer who urged the League to update their accounting system. This advice was ignored.

There were few fundraising activities during the early years of the war, and the one venture recorded in any detail seems to have been a slow process. At the annual general meeting on 16 May 1940 Dr Gerald Weigall, a medical doctor who specialised in paediatrics, stressed the importance of every hospital having a microscope, and £10 4s was donated. This was gradually increased, with various members of the Board adding small amounts at weekly intervals. When the microscope was finally bought in November 1941 there was still about £12 outstanding, and Mrs Lort Smith was asked if this could be paid out of her special fund. Fundraising in 1943 was more successful: a fete held at 'Myoora', Irving Road, Toorak by courtesy of Miss C. E. Masters raised £350, and a further £400 was collected by Mrs Lort Smith through various appeals.

Mrs Lort Smith gave generously to the hospital. In 1942 she paid £50 towards £71 required for the repainting of the hospital's exterior, and at the same time she donated several essential items to the hospital valued at nearly £20. She was extremely keen for a distemper hospital for dogs to be built and in September 1943 she bought a block of land in nearby Mary Street for this purpose. It was her dream that it should be built in memory of her sister, the late Miss Marion Montgomery. And when, in May 1944, the late Mrs A. M. White left the sum of £5000 to the hospital on condition that a satisfactory scheme for the extension of the hospital was approved by the trustees of her estate, it looked as though Mrs Lort Smith's dream would come true.

The annual general meeting for 1944 was held in May, shortly before the end of the war. It was a time of optimism for the League, with Lady Brookes being able to report that it was 'more solvent than it had been for many years'. The fete had raised £550, even more than the previous year. Mrs Lort Smith had promised to donate a further £1000 toward the building of the distemper hospital and the League was optimistic about being able to start building very soon.

The future was looking rosy.

Post-war years: 1946-1960

It might have been anticipated that the end of the war would have brought greater stability to the Lort Smith Hospital, but in fact staffing and financial difficulties meant that the next few years were full of crisis and turbulence. The one stable factor was the composition of the Board, and several founder members of the League were still very active. Some of the main protagonists were Mrs Lort Smith, until her death in 1956, Dame Mabel (formerly Lady) Brookes, Mrs Welsh, Mrs Cyril Trathan, Mrs Nelken, Mrs Perry and Mrs Claire Mackinnon.

When Dame Mabel was president she spent several months abroad every year, and during her absences the chair was usually taken by Mrs Trathan, Mrs Lort Smith, Mrs Charles Read or Mrs Welsh. Dame Mabel resigned from the Board in July 1951 because of her other commitments – at this time she was running for state parliament but did not win the seat. She was re-elected to the Board in March 1956, two months before the death of Mrs Lort Smith, and resumed the presidency which she held until her death in 1975.

Queuing for treatment in the early 1950s, *Unidentified newspaper, AWL scrapbook.*

Mrs Claire Mackinnon and Dame Mabel Brookes with their pets.
Photo courtesy of Mrs Jillian Gengoult Smith.

Mrs Lort Smith, *Herald,* October 1955, *AWL scrapbook.*

Mrs Lort Smith was elected president for the first time in 1951. In June 1953 she was awarded a commemorative Coronation medal, but she did not at any time receive any higher official recognition such as an OBE. Mr W. Weigall wrote a somewhat poignant letter to her on 3 June 1953 expressing his regret:

I really do think that you're entitled to something more than what 12,500 other people were thought worthy of, and, instead of saying to you how pleased I am I can only say that I am hopeful that all in due time your wonderful work for animals will get some proper recognition officially.

I think that the community recognises very fully what you have done, and you have certainly established in the shape of a monument something that will always go down as part, at any rate, of your memorial. May it be many many years, however, before you leave off adding to it and extending to it.

There were frequent tensions and divisions within the committee during these years, and stormy meetings. Several committee members threatened or offered to resign. In almost all instances the members did not follow through with their threats. However, Mrs Oswald Gibson did, and told the League in February 1952 that she wished the League all the success and progress it should achieve, 'providing it strives towards an undivided front'.

Unlike many organisations that welcome members because of the revenue and other types of support membership may attract, the Board of the Animal Welfare League have always been selective as to whom they would admit. Perhaps because members have seen it as a somewhat exclusive organisation, the Board could give the impression of being unwelcoming and unfriendly at their public functions. A League member, Mrs Weekes, wrote in September 1951 that she had tried to encourage friends to join the League and had invited them to functions such as the fete and the annual general meeting. However, they found the attitude toward them cold, and they left feeling unimpressed. Mrs Weekes said that she felt that it was in the 'interest of the League to give a welcome to the stranger'. The committee decided that they should wear sashes to distinguish themselves when they mingled with the guests: they hoped this 'may create a feeling of warmer hospitality', but sashes could also reinforce the image of higher rank and officialdom.

In 1945 the plan to build the distemper hospital was resurrected. Such a facility would not only provide treatment for large numbers of dogs with distemper, not currently provided for, but would also increase the amount of space available to treat other animals. Mrs A. M. White's £5000 bequest was shortly to become available, subject to the plans being approved. Mrs Lort Smith contacted the architect, Mr Leighton Irwin, to see if the new building could be started at the first available opportunity. Unfortunately the Department of Works and Housing turned down the application, advising that no permit could be granted at that time 'owing to the necessity to conserve the limited available resources for the erection of houses for families experiencing excessive hardship'.

In October 1952 the Board paid £1500 for the two-storey property immediately next door at 28 Villiers Street, which would allow them to expand northward at a later date. It cost £40 for the house to be demolished, but it meant that expansion of the hospital was now possible on the one site, and the Mary Street property was no longer the preferred place for building.

Urgent repairs were performed as required – for instance in 1948 the water pipes had corroded so badly that they all needed to be replaced, as did the floors in the kennels, and some minor renovations were made during the late 1940s and early 1950s. But the main changes to the hospital buildings were not started until 1958 with money raised from the Mrs Lort Smith Memorial fund. The land in Mary Street was sold for £8000 to help pay for the new building and Mrs White's bequest came into effect thirteen years after it had been made available.

For many years after the war staffing had its ups and downs. The day-to-day management of the hospital was delegated to the secretary/manager. In March 1946 Mr J. Gregor McGregor was appointed to the position. There had been other applicants but no others were considered because 'it was felt by the Committee that it was a post for a man'. Mr McGregor was a man, and he'd had experience in working in animal welfare in Palestine, so he would have appeared to be the ideal candidate. He resigned in August, however, and Ellie Sansom, who had been employed as registrar for twelve years, took over the position. Two years previously, in October 1944 the Board minutes had recorded a tribute to her long and valued service. Her close friend Anna Cressey was appointed as assistant secretary. They were both well liked and respected by staff and the committee tried unsuccessfully to induce them to remain when they announced that they were leaving in March 1952 to start their own business – a mixed grocery shop.

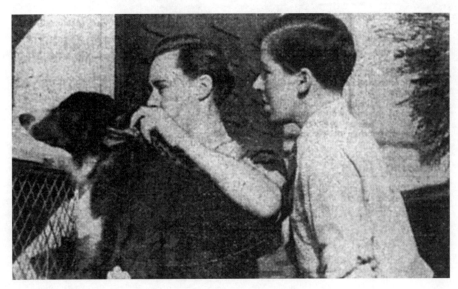

Ambulance drivers Miss Sansom and Mrs P. Williams, *The Sun*, 12 June, 1937, *Newspaper collection, State Library of Victoria.*

Miss Cumming was appointed secretary/manager in March 1952, but resigned in June and was replaced by Mr Beanland. Pat Ray, an ambulance driver at the time, when interviewed by Gerry Clarkson, described Mr Beanland as 'a funny man – he was always worried about money all the time'. Perhaps this was a useful quality because the hospital was continually running at a deficit, but not such a serious deficit as occurred after he left. He was replaced in November 1955 by Mr Moreton. Around this time the decision was made to replace the position of assistant secretary with a matron with a nursing background.

The recruitment and retention of veterinary staff was a constant problem in the post-war period. There was an exceptionally high turnover of vets and a large number of these had their contracts terminated because they did not conform to the exacting standards of the League. Few vets stayed for longer than one year, and in most cases it was considerably shorter. Two – Miss Elizabeth Harvey and Mr Richard Nemec – stand out in the length of time that they remained in employment, both staying for approximately four years.

Mr Spellman was appointed as a vet in August 1948. He was given a pay rise at his own request, and then started having ideas beyond his station, behaving as though he had been appointed to a managerial position. Resignation was offered to him – he refused. The Board then wrote to him giving him precise details of his employment as well as their expectations of him, but he continued to cause a good deal of disquiet, and the minutes of a meeting held on 5 April 1949 record that:

Mr Spellman, 1948, Photo: Lort Smith Animal Hospital.

> *gathering from the remarks and general attitude of members, Lady Brookes gained the opinion that there existed a lack of confidence in one of the League's veterinarians, and strongly recommended a sub-committee ... to ... thoroughly sift the whole question which according to Lady Brookes, is a most serious position, and whilst such a feeling exists smooth running of the Hospital cannot be maintained.*

The Board moved at a meeting on 24 May that they dispense with Mr Spellman's full-time services to the hospital, and he was offered part-time duties. Whilst he accepted the demotion to part-time employment he only agreed to do so from 23 November, when his existing contract expired. This was not satisfactory to the Board, and he was consequently given notice that his employment was to cease on 12 September 1949.

Mr McKenzie and Miss Harvey were both appointed in September: Mr McKenzie was chief veterinary officer, and Elizabeth Harvey (who had been the veterinary surgeon at the Lost Dogs' Home during the war years) was veterinary surgeon. When they were interviewed by the Board a month later they both said that they were happy with the running of the hospital and with their work. Concern was expressed about Miss Harvey's 'retiring facilities' so Mrs Lort Smith 'kindly offered to send from her home a table with mirror attached for Miss Harvey's use'. The Board were confident that the pair would be able to work well together and felt sure of their loyalty to the League.

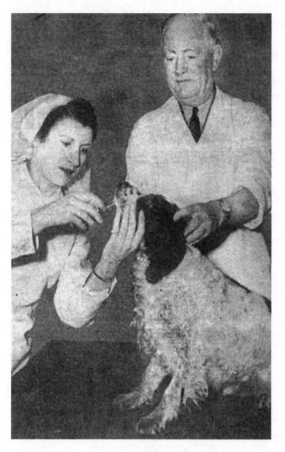

Jacko from Yarraville, having survived a snake bite, being fed by Nurse Edwards and Mr McKenzie, *Unidentified newspaper*, June 1949, *AWL scrapbook*.

Their optimism was unfounded: antagonism developed when Mr McKenzie complained about the distraction caused by Miss Harvey's dog Folly barking outside his surgery window. The Board said they were unable to intervene. Finally in October 1951 Mr McKenzie was sacked for taking four weeks' leave without permission, the second time he had done such a thing. Dr Duckett was appointed in his place at a salary of £1200, and Miss Harvey's salary was raised to £1000. Veterinary assistant Simon Fraser had assumed a good deal of Mr McKenzie's workload during the time he was away, and the Board gave him an honorarium of £25 and asked that a letter should be enclosed with the cheque stating that they regretted that the amount could not have been more but 'in effect it really was, as the many privileges enjoyed by Mr Fraser have increased in cost to such a degree, without further burden upon his private income'. In other words they were asking him to recognise their generosity in providing him with the perks of living on the premises. But this ignored the tremendous benefits his presence provided to both staff and animals since he was always on hand and willing to give after-hours treatment when required.

Miss Harvey worked for the hospital for nearly four years and was clearly well liked and respected by the Board. However, their close relationship seems to have gradually eroded and one incident may have brought to a head Miss Harvey's decision to resign. One of the privileges allowed to staff at this time was an afternoon off each week to go shopping, on the condition that they had not had time off for other reasons. In November 1953 Miss Harvey was censured by the

Board for apparently disobeying the secretary, Mr Beanland, and taking her shopping afternoon after absence at the dentist the previous Monday. On 1 December Miss Harvey protested to the Board that she had not been given the opportunity to explain the circumstances for her actions before being reprimanded. Two weeks later she appeared before the Board and told them that, because she had not been happy at the hospital for some time, and because she felt that she had lost all personal touch with the Board, she had decided to leave and devote more time to her private practice.

Miss Edmonstone, a recent graduate from Dubbo with four or five months' experience in private practice in Sydney, commenced veterinary duties in October 1954. A Board meeting was held on the following day and a

Miss Elizabeth Harvey and Miss Nan Muller, *The Argus* **19 December 1952,** *AWL scrapbook.*

motion was put that 'the Council insists that Staff Veterinary Surgeons carry out immunisations at the Hospital when veterinary services become normal'. A motion was also carried that 'the recommendation be adopted forthwith'. This decision was contrary to the policy of the Australian Veterinary Association.

Shortly after Miss Edmonstone started, the president, Mrs Lort Smith, had telephoned Mr Beanland to ask him to find out when Miss Edmonstone could do an immunisation for her. Miss Edmonstone was called to the phone and asked Mrs Lort Smith if she was to do the immunisation as a private job. The minutes recorded her reply and what followed:

Did Mrs Lort Smith realise that this is a Hospital for sick and injured animals. Did she realise what the reaction of the Veterinary Association would be? In all she was very rude. It was agreed that Miss Edmonstone should be brought before Council to give an explanation. Her explanation was on similar lines to that outlined by the President. She was also rude to Mrs Trathan and the Council generally and her attitude objectionable.

Following the interview the secretary was 'instructed to inform Miss Edmonstone of the Council's complete surprise at her whole attitude apart from her views regarding immunisation and that an apology is due to the President and Members of Council'. The minutes of the next meeting recorded that Miss Edmonstone, on being interviewed, 'had expressed regret as she had no intention of being rude'. A motion was passed that the matter be allowed to lapse. Miss Edmonstone did not remain at the hospital for long – she resigned early in 1955.

The League had an ambivalent attitude to neutering and immunising animals. Both operations were obviously not treating sick animals, one of the clear guidelines set down by the League, but on the other hand were performed in the best interests of the animals, and they provided much-needed income. The last recorded policy decision regarding neutering had been made in 1942: the procedure was not to be performed in the hospital. There was no consistent policy during the 1950s and the Board tended to yoyo between encouraging the procedure and forbidding it. When in September 1952 it was suggested that Dr Duckett undertake a few spaying operations each week he refused because 'this was what he termed a luxury operation and he would not cut across private practice'. In August 1955 Mr Nemec was asked if he would carry out spays to help increase revenue, but he said he would do so only in exceptional circumstances. Then in 1958, when the financial situation was critical, the Board decided that no spays were to be performed.

On the whole vets who were employed in the later years of the 1950s caused fewer problems, although there were some complaints of lateness and of unauthorised use of the telephone, and in June 1958 the vets Mr Meldrum and Mr Benaradsky were reprimanded by the president for unprofessional conduct on hospital premises. A number of vets worked at the hospital as locums or in the night clinic during this time including Dr Arminski, Dr Wiseman, Mr Meldrum, Dr Blashki and Dr Kent.

Whilst the veterinary staff changed frequently during this period, Simon Fraser provided the hospital with the consistency and professional expertise which was tremendously important. Staff often sought his advice, and he was highly respected by everyone who had contact with him, and as already mentioned he was extremely generous in giving his own time to treat animals in need. It is interesting that in all his years of work no criticism of his practice was ever recorded by any of the scores of vets he worked with. His dedication did not go unrecognised. On 22 January 1951 Lady Brookes told a Board meeting about the service Mr Fraser had rendered to her 'little Peke', and suggested that, in view of the enormous amount he did after hours to relieve suffering, the Council should, as a gesture of appreciation, give him a cheque for £50 before he went on his holiday.

Simon and Nell Fraser are remembered for the support and encouragement they gave to their colleagues in many tangible ways. For instance, at the end of a busy week they would prepare food and provide an environment where staff could wind down and relax. This helped to foster the sense of camaraderie commented on by several past employees of the time.

Tabby cat (hospital patient); Biddy (hospital dog); Terrier belonging to the relief secretary; Folly (Miss Harvey's dog); Smoky (hospital cat); Chicquita (Mrs Pat Jarrett's dog); Revel (dog belonging to ambulance driver Miss Helen Wreford), *Photo: Lort Smith Animal Hospital.*

Dr Arminski, a locum vet employed at the hospital, suggested in January 1954 that the Veterinary Board should be asked to give Simon Fraser a licence to practise, taking into account his exceptional ability. The Board received this suggestion enthusiastically and agreed to pursue the matter but there is no record of any outcome. Most veterinary surgeons took a lenient view of the work done by Simon Fraser (which was technically illegal as he was not licensed) and were prepared to supervise him when no qualified vet was available. Dr Duckett, however, refused to make such a concession, so that when Miss Harvey took her four weeks' annual leave she had to be replaced by a locum vet.

The hospital kept two dogs as pets, Biddy and Twinkle, as well as two cats, Smoky and Scarlet. In April 1953 the Board ordered that these were the only animals, apart from Miss Harvey's dog Folly, to be allowed on the hospital premises other than patients.

Pat Jarrett (née West Lau) remembers that Smoky was a particular favourite of one of the Board members, Mrs Onslow, who used to feed the cat rabbit stew.

Pat Jarrett was employed as an ambulance driver toward the end of the 1940s and in the early 1950s and is one of three non-medical staff who have shared their memories of the hospital during this period. Pat recalled how she loved the work at the hospital because it was so animal focused. She describes it as a 'splendid place' and 'genuine'. Staff were encouraged to do what needed to be done. There was a very real commitment to the animals that were brought in for treatment or were strays, and this meant that staff were given a lot of latitude and flexibility in their work. All the staff worked hard to minimise the waiting period, and three-quarters of an hour was considered a long wait. X-rays were done on the spot by Simon Fraser and veterinary nurse Nan Muller, another dedicated and highly skilled staff member. But Pat was also aware of the darker side of the work, and found the sadness so overwhelming that on a couple of occasions she had to take time off from her work.

Pat would work at weekends whenever she could. One regular occurrence was a phone call from Mrs Lort Smith, who, although she knew Pat personally because Pat had visited her home, always asked the same series of questions and gave the same retort:

Pat:	*Lort Smith Hospital. Can I help you?*
Caller:	*What's your name and how long have you been working for the League?*
Pat:	*Oh! Good morning, Mrs Lort. It's Pat and I've been working for the League for two years.*
Mrs Lort Smith:	*Pat who?*
Pat:	*Pat West Lau.*
Mrs Lort Smith:	*How do you like working for the League?*
Pat:	*Very much. I love my job. It's a very rewarding experience.*
Mrs Lort Smith:	*Good. Well then, keep the flag flying!*

In 1949 the *Australian Woman's Day* ran an article on people who were working on Christmas Day, and it briefly outlined Pat's work and included this photograph:

Pat got to know one particular stray, which she recognised as a 'professional' and a frequenter of the Queen Victoria Market. One day she was called to an emergency outside Myer's city store and found a small Kelpie-cross on the footpath surrounded by a clutch of concerned people. She noticed as she loaded him into her small DKW car, which was used as an ambulance around the city area, that he had conveniently lain down over the hot air vent. Rather than take him to hospital she gave him a lift 'home'! Pat also remembers that:

Mrs Pat Jarrett with her dog, *Woman's Day,* **19 December 1949,** *AWL scrapbook.*

The hospital kennels for dog inpatients consisted of a series of pens housed in a long building on the left – very warm, heated by 'pot-belly' stove, fuelled by coke and briquettes supplied by the SEC, and generously carted by Lou Arthur's trucks. Mr Arthur was a great supporter of Mrs Lort, and always ready when such transport was needed. Also the rabbit exporters – Simmonds & Co in Blackwood Street, always very generous with free rabbits, which we cooked for our cat inmates. Very good people. We had quite a lot of dogs sent from the country, patients and others for homes, always well received by Mr Davies at 'Inward Parcels!!!' Spencer Street. Always very helpful ... Alas, no such service exists in our enlightened community.

Pat was occasionally asked into the Board meetings to undertake a particular task. She remembers when she was asked to take in a kindle of kittens. Mrs Oswald Gibson was a lady of very small stature who used to wear large and very splendid hats which gave her an air of great superiority. Pat remembers that on one occasion Mrs Gibson gave the other Board members a demonstration of how to tell the sex of kittens by passing some silken thread through a gold wedding ring and dangling it over a kitten. The sex was determined according to the direction in which the ring circulated (clockwise or anti-clockwise) Pat cannot remember the significance of each. Pat was herself skilled in determining the sex of young kittens, and what she does remember is that Mrs Gibson invariably got it right!

Pat was very keen on horses, and on one occasion the rag-and-bone man who travelled around North Melbourne had an accident and his horse had to be brought to the Lort Smith. Pat was eager to look after the horse and went to the Queen Victoria Market to buy hay and straw for him. Unfortunately his stay was short, and he was soon taken by someone from the RSPCA to the Rest Home for Horses at Tally Ho.

Another incident Pat remembers well also concerned horses. One of her weekend jobs was to take the dead bodies to the knackery beside the Maribyrnong River for disposal. After the war the availability of fuel meant that many draught horses were no longer needed as businesses went back to using motorised transport. Pat noticed that there were a large number of horses crammed into appalling conditions waiting for slaughter and looking unhappy and scared. She reported this to Miss Sansom, who told the Board. Pat was asked to accompany Board member Joan Richmond to the knackery so Joan could photograph the conditions. The best vantage point was from the river itself, so the pair hired a dinghy from a nearby firm of boat builders and Pat was given the task of rowing – not a skill she had developed or which came naturally to her but she managed somehow with some help from Joan. They had to navigate a corner of the river before they reached their destination, and there they found knackery workers lined up along the bank. When they saw the huge press-type camera Joan was wielding they shouted obscenities at the pair. Pat was used to hearing such language so she was more embarrassed for Joan than for herself. Joan was obviously 'to the manor born', handsome and very sophisticated. However, she had also lived a 'fast' life so on reflection Pat believes that she would not have been surprised or shocked by the obscenities hurled at them. The photographs were published in the press, and Pat believes that they helped to relieve the plight of these unfortunate animals.

Miss Joan Richmond, *The Age*, August 2000.

According to her obituary in *The Age* on 16 August 2000 Joan, who was born in 1905, was given a former racehorse when she was eighteen, which she trained herself and raced successfully at meetings around Benalla. She was furious when a ban against women jockeys was introduced so she switched to motor racing, finishing fifth in the Australian Grand Prix at Phillip Island in 1931. In the same year she drove overland to Europe where she competed in the Monte Carlo rally. She continued a career in motor racing in the UK as a professional rally driver and was the first woman to win an international race. She worked during the war for the De Havilland Aircraft factory but afterwards she returned to Australia where she took up the cause of animal welfare.

To quote from a letter from Pat Jarrett:

The outstanding memory I have personally of Lort Smith was that we all loved our job, took it very seriously, and made sure we followed the golden rule – the animals came first! A great bunch of people, all out to achieve the same result. Hours worked were unimportant-in my case, I was always early for work! Mr Budd the Yard Man was always there first, and opened up the gates. He was a great old boy.

Hospital ambulance, 1948,
Unidentified newspaper,
AWL scrapbook.

Another ambulance driver, Pat Ray, who worked in the late 1940s, remembers taking animal carcasses to the knackery, known also as the 'boiling down works', at the weekend. She remembers that on the Saturday she was married this was her last job before going home to get bathed and changed. Pat Ray also remembers collecting a dog from a man with a flower stall in the city; the owner told her that the dog was to have his tonsils out. When she told the vet of the dog's complaint, he started to shave his patient's nether regions. Pat thought the vet had not understood and reiterated that it was his tonsils which needed to be operated on. She was told that for a dog 'to have his tonsils out' was a common way to refer to castration.

Pat Ray also remembers being reprimanded by Board member Mrs Cyril Trathan who, once driving behind her, saw her blond hair blowing in the wind. The Board had very high expectations of staff conduct and standard of dress, including the length of hair, and several times it ruled that hair should not be worn below the collar, or should be tied back.

Mrs Phyllis (Phyl) Taylor started work as a receptionist in 1956. This was shortly before Mrs Lort Smith died. She saw her on one occasion when she visited the hospital but did not speak to her. Phyl knew little about animals and she found her first few weeks overwhelming – there were so many unexpected things that happened and she felt that she was having to shoulder a great deal of responsibility. She would burst into tears when she got home and frequently lost her appetite.

At that time animals were not immunised or neutered. As a general rule all stray females had to be put down because of the limited accommodation, although the odd ones were kept that might go to homes. Some non-veterinary staff were expected to put animals to sleep, although Phyl never did.

When she first started there were only two vets and the hospital was open from 9 am to 5 pm on weekdays and from 9 am to 12 noon on Saturdays. Phyl used to work on reception but she would help out with other duties, and would often relieve over the lunch break and take calls including ambulance bookings. There was no way of contacting drivers in an emergency unless it was known that one of the clients being called on had a telephone. She often felt powerless to help, particularly if a call came in at the end of the day and no ambulance was contactable. Phyl remembers the job as being one of hard work and constant anxiety but she learnt to cope.

Sometimes she relieved in the evenings, when the clinic would be open from 5-9 pm. She found it scary having to be responsible for the money and for locking up after the clinic finished. With inadequate lighting, she had to check the dogs in the kennel and lock the gates. Sometimes the local down-and-outs used to sneak into the waiting bays to find somewhere warm to sleep.

In August 1958 Mr Moreton, secretary/manager, told the Board that he had been unable to find a satisfactory accounts clerk, and recommended that the work be shared between himself, Mrs Taylor and another clerical worker, Miss Stewart. He suggested that Mrs Taylor and Miss Stewart should be given a pay rise of thirty shillings a week each and this would save about £400 per annum in the wages of a clerk. This promotion enabled Phyl to expand her repertoire of skills, and although she never learnt to type she was ultimately promoted to hospital secretary.

Towards the middle of the 1950s the Board was grappling with severe financial difficulties. Four men offered their services to form a finance advisory committee: the treasurer Mr Treloar; the legal adviser Mr George Crowther; Mr Charles Booth and Mr H. Rushton, who was soon replaced by Mr Jack S. Smith (later a Professor at the University of Melbourne). The committee was set up in March 1956 and shortly afterwards the members were elected to the Board, although their attendance was spasmodic, usually when important financial matters were to be discussed. Mr Moreton was instructed to cooperate with the committee in all aspects of its work, and keep it up to date with all financial matters. One of the initiatives proposed by the finance committee was the introduction of a suitable budget control system.

The Board members demonstrated an ambivalence to the committee: they wanted and valued their opinions but they also wanted the freedom to act as they thought fit. They frequently ignored or gave only lip service to any uncomfortable advice. Their arguments were based on emotion rather than logic. It was an uneasy relationship and one cannot but wonder at the dedication and patience of the four men who devoted so much time and expertise to the committee with very little thanks.

Charles Booth (later Sir Charles) was a managing director of Australian Paper Manufacturers and a director of the Bankers and Traders Insurance Co. Ltd. He became involved in the financial management of the hospital in the mid 1950s. It is likely that he was a friend of Sir Norman Brookes as they were both associated with the paper mills. He was a member of the Board for ten years and resigned in March 1966 although he continued as a member of the finance advisory committee until his death in July 1970.

George O'Dell Crowther was a solicitor in the firm of Weigall and Crowther, and took over from Mr Weigall as honorary solicitor in the late 1940s. In March 1966 he resigned from the Board but said that he was happy to continue as a member of the finance advisory committee.

He gave free legal advice to the League, and in return was given free treatment at the hospital for his poodles. His firm also acted for the League at considerably reduced rates. In June 1981 the Board congratulated him on being awarded the MBE and also took the opportunity to thank him for his free legal advice.

He was badly crippled with polio as a child, and walking was difficult for him. He died on 2 June 1993. The July Board meeting moved that 'the services of Mr Crowther to the League were most appreciated and that his work be recorded'. Several committee members attended his funeral.

The Board was faced with a dilemma, having set their minds once again on building a distemper hospital. The Mary Street site which Mrs Lort Smith had donated to the League in the mid 1940s was available but was no longer ideal. The recently purchased two-storey house adjacent to the hospital was a more convenient location for any new building. But all the time the costs of running their existing hospital were rising steeply, the hospital faced an increasing deficit every year and there were other problems needing to be addressed. In October 1955 Dame Mabel submitted a report from Mr Treloar recommending that 'any expenditure on building schemes should be suspended until such time as we had set our house in order'.

This did not stop Mrs Lort Smith from pursuing the matter. She was in poor health but would have been keen for work on the extension to have begun while she was still around to superintend the building. It is likely that she took matters into her own hands, and early in July 1956 Leighton Irwin sent plans of some proposed hospital extensions to Mrs Lort Smith. Unfortunately she died a few days after receiving them and although one abortive attempt was made to get the project under way it was in fact another two years before the Board was in the position to make the decision to extend the hospital.

The problem which diverted the Board from the building program was how to run the night clinic on a viable basis. It was beset not only by financial difficulties but also by staffing problems. There is no record of when the night clinic, which had been running at the end of the 1940s, had closed down, but it was reopened in January 1957, at first from Monday to Thursday from 6-8 pm, but later when staffing became difficult, on Mondays and Wednesdays only. The two vets, Mr Nemec and Mr Morath, staffed the night clinic in addition to the day clinic but when this became too onerous they told the Board that they would continue only until another vet was found. When hiring another vet proved impossible the clinic was forced to close in April. The finance advisory committee's first job was to advise how the night service could continue to operate, even if this meant curtailing other areas of operation.

The finance advisory committee made some interim suggestions, setting out guidelines under which the night service should operate. It was calculated that a night clinic would lose about £600 per annum if paid labour was used, so it was suggested that a paid vet be appointed but that the positions of vet assistant and cashier be filled by voluntary workers. Mr Turnbull, who had already been interviewed for the position of night clinic vet by the Board and recommended for appointment, was asked to start work as soon as possible, and an attempt was made to find voluntary helpers.

The night clinic reopened on 5 August 1957, with Mr Turnbull in charge. Not all the assistance provided was voluntary. Instead the positions of cashier and vet assistant were combined to save money. Nell Fraser agreed to act as pharmacist without extra payment. Mr Turnbull's employment lasted for less than one week. His services were terminated when on 13 August, he reported for duty one-and-a-half hours late, and 'not in a condition to carry out his duties'. Mr Morath took over the clinic again on a temporary basis, and Mr Harbord was engaged from 19 August.

In June 1957 finance committee member Mr Rushton, to help the Board in its planning, arranged for a team of 'efficiency experts' to report on the hospital's operation. Meanwhile, unknown to the finance advisory committee, the Board and the architectural firm of Leighton Irwin had continued to develop the plans which had been provided to Mrs Lort Smith for the hospital extension and on 2 July the Board put the work out to tender. This was clearly not acceptable to the finance advisory committee which insisted that all matters of capital expenditure and the appointment of veterinary staff should have its prior approval. They asked for and were successful in having the tendering process stopped, but this is a typical example of the almost impossible conditions under which the finance advisory committee had to work. The Board was effectively presenting them with a double bind by saying 'we will do what you say, but we will also do whatever we want to do'.

The final report of the finance committee, presented to the Board in mid September 1957, suggested that the best way to ensure the hospital's future was for it to expand. It recommended that the night and weekend clinic should attempt to break even or make a profit, that the League promote itself with more publicity, and in particular increase the number of treatments performed since this was the most profitable side of its work. The area of ambulance cover should be extended with the aim of each ambulance handling fifteen animals per day. The charge for inpatients should be increased by 60% and a simple monthly control system introduced so that the League could monitor its financial affairs.

The Board agreed to raise fees for inpatients by 33% instead of the recommended 60%; the area covered by ambulance was extended; and three sub-committees were set up to work on promotion, the auxiliaries and hospital management. These subcommittees do not appear to have been particularly active or to have made a significant difference.

By the end of 1957 the amount of day-time work had increased and a new vet, Mr Benaradsky, was appointed from the start of the following year. It was reported that the financial situation had improved. The total number of cases handled had increased by 22.7%, and the percentage of inpatients by 42.47%, while the number of cases brought in by two ambulances were 5976 against 5886 brought in by three ambulances in 1956. The overdraft had been liquidated and there was a small balance in hand at the end of the year. There had been an operating surplus of £2596 as opposed to a deficit of £1914 the previous year. The night and weekend clinic had also made a profit of £890 in approximately four months and the pharmacy had just about broken even. Mr Moreton was given an ex gratia payment as an expression of the Board's gratitude. In June 1958 the Board, without the approval of the finance committee, appointed Mr Meldrum as an additional night-clinic vet.

Unfortunately it was discovered in the following month that, whether due to the previous balance being estimated by an over-optimistic accounting process, a sudden downturn in trading, or the overspending of the Board on capital items, by the end of July 1958 the hospital was again running at a serious deficit. Revenue was reported to be down by £2015 and expenditure up by £1001. The finance advisory committee was 'deeply concerned with this state of affairs', and in particular the fact that the Board had once again taken unilateral action in appointing a new vet. The committee told the Board that Mr Meldrum's appointment could not be justified and asked that his permanent position cease from 3 September.

The finance committee complained that a large part of the overall deficit was caused by non-adherence to the budget. Not only had the salary budget been exceeded, but the Board had bought a new ambulance in spite of the hospital having failed to achieve the budgeted income from the existing ambulance fleet. The Board had decided to buy the ambulance out of the proceeds of the annual fete, and had not therefore thought it necessary to consult the committee. They had not factored into their decision-making the additional running costs. The committee concluded:

It is the view of the committee that unless the operation of the League be kept closely in line with the annual budget it could well find that in the very near future its financial situation would be very precarious.

But the Board continued to ignore the advice of the committee when it decided, in September 1958, not to adopt the committee's recommendation that fees be raised because 'this was directly opposed to the aims and aspirations of the founder of this Hospital'. Such decisions did nothing to help keep the hospital solvent. In February 1959 the Board was told by the committee that the loss for 1958 was approximately £7700 (actually £6897) whilst a loss of £4650 had been budgeted for, and they were advised that they 'should endeavour to raise money by all other means in [their] power'.

Staff pay and conditions were areas where the Board did generally exercise restraint. Pay rises were significantly less than were asked for, or a one-off bonus was given instead. The vets were frequently dissatisfied with their pay and were constantly asking for more money. In August 1957 Mr Crowther told the Board that 'the present rates of pay were quite high enough' but this view was obviously not shared by the vets. Mr Benaradsky and Mr Morath both gave notice after a meeting with Dame Mabel Brookes, and left in November 1958.

There followed a 100% turnover of veterinary staff within the space of about four months. In October Mr Nemec was given the position of senior surgeon and an increase of £100 but he resigned in January 1959. Mr Gannon was appointed in November and Mr Tudhope was appointed day-clinic vet from 4 January 1959 at a salary of £1650. A new vet, Mr Pulvirenti, started in January 1959 on a salary of £1550 and brought some stability to the hospital.

The Board applied their staffing policies rigorously on most occasions, although it has already been demonstrated that in some instances – for example bonuses paid to Simon Fraser – they exercised flexibility. In October 1956 Mrs Ferguson, a long-serving staff member, fell ill and asked if her pay could continue while she was off work. The Board refused, on the grounds that it would set a precedent, but her wages were paid personally by Mrs Sadie Howe.

Sadie Howe joined the Board in 1955. Her contribution to the hospital was valued and she was made an honorary office bearer in April 1965. She replaced Dame Mabel Brookes as president in 1975, a position she held for fifteen years, until her resignation in 1989, the same year that she was awarded the Order of Australia Medal for 'service to the community'.

Sadie Howe with Dr McCaughey at Government House after she received the Order of Australia, 1989, *Photo: Lort Smith Animal Hospital.*

When she was young Sadie used to accompany Mrs Lort Smith in her horse and trap. Mrs Lort Smith always insisted on leaving home with plenty of time to spare before an appointment. 'This was to allow time for "incidents", which, with Mrs Lort Smith at the helm, were always plentiful, from picking up a stray dog to berating a man whipping his horse.'

Sadie had an excellent grasp of finances and investments and she played a major part in putting the hospital in a sound financial position. She continued to have a significant role in the hospital's investment policy until her retirement. She was also tireless in her approach to fundraising, particularly in seeking bequests. She is said to have visited likely people with a cake in one hand and will forms in the other – but insisted that the gift of cake was of little monetary value in case the recipient believed that it was being paid for from hospital funds! In fact the money came from her own pocket.

Pat Patience tells an amusing story of how she and Phyl Taylor waited for Sadie outside the old Commonwealth Buildings where she had gone to renew her passport in readiness for a trip to India to visit a friend who was a maharajah. The young man who interviewed her commented that there were three names on her file not including her maiden name. Sadie replied, 'Well, I have been married three times,' which drew the response, 'Have you really?' Sadie came out with 'Well, I haven't always bloody well looked like this!'

Pat also told of Sadie's generosity in opening her home in Brighton for card parties, mannequin parades and tennis parties. She paid for all the catering, which was done on a grand scale. Her invited friends always ended up in the kitchen putting food on plates – 'but no one objected as Sadie herself worked non-stop.' Her cook used to make dozens of sponges and it was the helpers' job to ice and decorate them. When it came time to fill them with cream Sadie would keep a

sharp watch on how much cream was being used and it was never enough. Her catch-cry was 'More cream! More cream!'

Pat concludes: 'The Lort Smith will never see the likes of Sadie Howe again. The years she gave of her time, money, energy should never be forgotten. She was the most generous of human beings.'

In August 1977 Sadie Howe received a silver jubilee medal to commemorate the ascension of Queen Elizabeth II to the throne.

Sadie Howe, Elizabeth Osborne and Pat Patience, 1980s, *Photo: Lort Smith Animal Hospital.*

She died on 17 March 2001. Alan Lawther wrote in a valedictory tribute:

She was a larger than life character: a spade was a spade — the message came straight from the shoulder and with an unwavering gaze. She added to the world of those she met. We have all benefited by her life.

Fundraising and donations enabled the League to survive during these years. Although various suggestions were made about fundraising events immediately after the war, these were not pursued. The Board was very busy dealing with problems concerning one of its auxiliaries in Ringwood which was deeply divided. Many of the League's members were also very involved in the anti-cruelty campaign which is discussed in chapter ten. But the community continued to give open-handedly. One generous donation of £5000 was made in October 1954 by Lady Mary Herring, the daughter of Lady Lyle, on behalf of the family.

Mrs Mackinnon was one of the most stalwart fundraisers during the 1950s. On 22 August 1952 she organised a mannequin parade at Menzies Hotel with her friend, Lillian Wightman, the owner of Le Louvre, a Melbourne establishment which still exists today. Madame La Motte, a well-known milliner, also paraded her hats. Mrs Mackinnon invited over 100 people to Menzies Hotel to discuss the arrangements for the fashion parade, and one of the suggestions was that staff from the hospital should attend the parade with their own pets. A second fashion parade organised by Mrs Mackinnon was held in October 1954 at the same venue and raised £1735.

Glamour and glitter support the
Animal Welfare League, *The Argus*,
23 August 1952, *AWL scrapbook*.

Miss Lillian Wightman, Mrs Mackinnon
and Georgina Weir, *The Age* 28 February
1974, *AWL scrapbook*.

Claire Mackinnon (née Adams) was an American actress who married Scobie Mackinnon, an extremely wealthy Western District grazier, soon after they met in the USA. The Mackinnon Stakes, run during the Melbourne Cup carnival, is named after Scobie's father. Current Board member David White knew her well, and says that Scobie and Claire adored each other. They had no children but shared an interest in horse racing. On their way from the USA to Australia they had a honeymoon in the UK and Scobie bought Claire a Rolls Royce as a wedding present. They had a property near Skipton in the western district of Victoria. Claire was treated with some suspicion when she first arrived because of her life on the stage, but when she was taken up by Mrs Jess Russell, a member of the Board and a popular socialite, people could not have been more hospitable. She became a popular and respected member of the Board.

She was extremely generous and was constantly making donations to the hospital, often providing an item which was badly needed. Phyl Taylor remembers the warmth and generosity she extended to her on a personal basis, and when she visited her at Skipton Mrs Mackinnon made her feel particularly welcome by remaining physically close to her when well-known people, including Lady Bolte, wife of Premier Henry Bolte, were present.

A stray golden cocker spaniel was brought to the hospital in May 1952 with an eye injury. Mrs Lort Smith ordered that the dog be destroyed, but when Dr Duckett could not bring himself to do so Mrs Mackinnon donated £2 to cover the expenses of continuing to look after the dog, and an advertisement was placed in the newspaper. The owner was traced and it was resolved that in future every attempt be made to find the owners of stray dogs brought to the hospital.

Mrs Mackinnon used her connections to organise fundraising events for the League. The Board minutes described her as 'an invaluable worker in our cause and always expressed her happiness in doing so'. She would always stop to help an animal in distress, and Phyl Taylor remembers that if a dog was injured she would assist even if she were being driven to a function in full evening dress, and she was well known around the city for this. Mrs Mackinnon's positive attitude is demonstrated by occasions when she suggested the reframing of negative statements into positive ones: as an example, a notice on the hospital verandah which said 'Dogs prohibited unless controlled by leash' was replaced with 'Dogs must be controlled by leash'.

When in 1957 the finance committee refused to allow essential work to commence on the waiting areas Mrs Mackinnon paid for the work to be done herself as a memorial to her late father, Stanley Adams.

When she died, a sale of her clothing was held in the Lower Melbourne Town Hall in aid of the League. David White remembers that two or three trestles were just given up to gloves. A trust fund set up after her death made several generous donations to the hospital in the mid-1980s when the rebuilding program was taking place.

The Lort Smith Memorial Appeal opened shortly after Louisa died in June 1956. About eighty people met at Dame Mabel Brookes' home on 3 September to plan the appeal. Mr Crowther was elected chairman and Mr Treloar treasurer. A target of £20,000 was set, but this was later reduced to £10,000. Dame Mabel held unsuccessful discussions with the federal treasurer about making the contributions tax deductible. Today this remains the stance of the government.

Lady Brooks, wife of Victoria's then Governor, Sir Dallas Brooks, and patroness of the hospital, agreed to be appeal president. The sum of £2000 had already been raised between September and the official appeal opening at Dame Mabel's house, 'Kurneh', on 26 February 1957.

A very successful dinner dance with a band and three singers had been organised by Mrs Mackinnon at Menzies Hotel on 22 October the previous year. Sir Dallas and Lady Brooks attended and it was said that they both enjoyed themselves. It raised approximately £550. Other events in 1956 included the showing of the play 'The Reluctant Debutante' on 5 October, and a fancy-dress ball. Various future fundraising events were advertised at the official opening-a luncheon to be held by the Raveloe Auxiliary on 14 March 1957, the Lort-Smith-Montgomery Ball to be held on 21 June at the Malvern Town Hall, a fete in October at Dame Mabel's Frankston home, 'Cliff House', and a travel film night organised by Mrs Adam.

Sir Dallas and Lady Brooks at the opening of the hospital extension, *The Sun,* 17 March 1960, *Newspaper Collection, State Library of Victoria.*

The raffle of a deep freeze valued at £150 (tickets sold for two shillings) which was donated by Charles Booth raised £118 18s. The raffle was drawn on 12 January 1957 at the annual fete held at 'Cliff House'. Lady Budge also donated two tickets to the Olympic Games to be raffled.

It seems that, after the initial enthusiasm and flurry of activity, the League's fundraising activities gradually ran out of puff. In July 1957 the hospital secretary, Mr Moreton, wrote to Dame Mabel in London with hospital news and mentioned that 'the Appeal has hung fire a little of late'. In the end the appeal raised £11,000.

Final plans for the hospital extension, completed by Mr Grouse of Leighton Irwin & Co., were agreed to by the Board in November 1958. A. Yates and Partners won the tender with a price of £16,670. The work was to be completed in sixteen weeks. The building process seems to have been trouble-free and completed on time.

The hospital extension was opened by Sir Dallas Brooks on 16 March 1960. It was thirty years and five days since the first Animal Welfare League clinic had been opened by Lord Somers and during those years the League had overcome many problems. It would have been a proud moment when the new hospital was finally declared open, but there could have been no doubt in the minds of the Board that there were fresh difficulties and challenges awaiting them.

Keeping afloat: 1960-1979

The years from 1960 to 1979 were probably the most difficult in the history of the hospital as the Board tried to keep it afloat. The evidence seems to suggest that, in its desire to be in control, the Board was too concerned with detail to be able to grasp the big picture or to learn from its mistakes or from the advice of others. So it struggled through years of financial and staff crises and at times it was only the generosity of individual Board members and benefactors that kept the hospital solvent.

1960 began with a repetition of the previous year's events when an initial perusal of the end-of-year accounts gave an utterly misleading picture of the financial situation. On 9 January 1960 Dame Mabel congratulated those concerned on achieving an excellent surplus instead of the budgeted deficit. But on further examination the hospital was found to have had a serious deficit of £6982 for the year 1959 and this was likely to rise steeply during the coming year. So in March 1960 the Board was confronted with another serious but unforeseen financial crisis.

Inflation was rising. There was pressure for wage increases. The list of essential repairs included a leaking roof that could not be easily fixed. Since a replacement roof would cost £360 it was decided to defer taking action. On 3 May the bank agreed to extend the overdraft to £5000 for three months only but as it already stood at £4939 it was necessary to hold over some bills requiring payment. Some drastic action was required if the hospital was to remain solvent. It was decided to close the clinic at nights and on public holidays and to reduce the number of ambulance drivers from three to two. Locums were to be employed at the weekend clinic only if it was impossible to staff it from the permanent staff. The deficit for 1960 was £8775, although the number of patients seen during the year had risen to 30,944, a 9.6% increase.

The decision to close the night and weekend clinic was rescinded at the next meeting, and the hospital and the Australian Veterinary

Association began some serious negotiations which would have handed the organisation of the emergency service to the AVA. Details of these discussions are given in chapter ten, but the final outcome was that the League continued to run the service.

Dr Justin Barker was employed as a vet at the beginning of the 1960s and Dr Gerry Clarkson has recorded Dr Barker's reminiscences of the Board which he described as autocratic and demonstrating 'incredible condescension'. He attributed this mainly to the grand personage of Dame Mabel Brookes. She was good for the 'Lorty' network, so people went along with this hierarchical 'forelock tugging' state of affairs. The big event was the monthly inspection by the committee:

> *There may have been 30 people in the waiting bays, but in the same way that the Melbourne Cup stops Australia, so the inspection of the Committee stopped the Lort Smith. The sequence of events on the appointed day followed these lines. Someone would call out – 'they're on their way!' The next thing you knew a flotilla of women with coiffeured Toorak hair styles would swarm into the surgery and inspect everything from soap holders to auroscopes. Some inappropriate questions would be asked and then they would float out en masse, leaving you to consult for the remainder of the day in a faintly scented atmosphere.*

The Board expected the hospital to maintain a high level of formality and in January 1965 staff were asked to address vets by their surnames while on duty or within the hospital. The Board expected to exercise control over all aspects of hospital management, and demanded that its policy take precedence even over a vet's professional judgement.

Pettiness and rivalry between Board members continued during these years and into the 1970s. Joan Sturzaker recalls how in November 1974 she was nominated to the Board by Vena Davey and Alison Lemon but she withdrew her nomination when the Board suddenly and with a good deal of argument decided to adopt a secret ballot in an attempt to prevent Joan's election. The opposition to her nomination stemmed from the antagonism between two of the Board members, Vena Davey and Ormé Patterson. Ormé did all she could to block Joan's election because she had been proposed by Vena.

When David White was elected to the Board in September 1976 (he was the first member to be elected by secret ballot) they met twice a month. David had worked in industrial relations in licensed clubs for about fifteen years so he brought a good deal of experience to the position. It was through his friendship with Joyce Barker, the League's vice-president, that he first became involved with the Lort Smith. She encouraged him to join the Board because she was aware that Professor Jack Smith wanted to retire and she felt that David would bring valuable financial experience to the Board. He is an Associate of the Australian Society of Accountants and as the chairman of the Board he upheld the traditional values and modus operandi of the League.

David remembers that Board meetings were conducted with great formality, with everyone having their designated seats. Tea and sandwiches were served. Most of the women were heavy smokers. Amongst the 'old guard' society women who were involved with the hospital was its president, Ormé Patterson, wife of Gerald Patterson, a well-known tennis player and nephew of Dame Nellie Melba. Judith Cable had a long association with the hospital. Her mother, Mrs U. J. Nicholas, was an early member of the Board, and immediately after she left school Judith volunteered to drive the hospital ambulance, which she did for a short time in the early 1930s. She served on the Board between 1939 and 1944 after her first marriage to Keith Halley, and also drove a Red Cross Ambulance as a part of the war effort. After her second marriage she joined the Board for a second time from 1970 until 1983, this time with the name Judith Cable.

Dr Alan Lawther joined the hospital on 30 October 1962 and played a very significant part in its future. He was described by his colleague, Dr Gerry Clarkson, as one of the 'superstars' of the Lort Smith Animal Hospital because of his almost continuous involvement over forty years. He was always concerned to balance the local community needs for veterinary care with those of his veterinary colleagues who were trying to make a living in private practice and he would on occasion take the Board to task when he felt that the balance was out of kilter. He resigned from full-time employment in October 1968 when he set up his own clinic.

Dr Alan Lawther's description of the Board differs slightly from that of Justin Barker in that he emphasises their hard work and dedication:

The Hospital, in common with many other civic institutions, was guided by a Board of socially prominent women. The President of the League was Dame Mabel Brookes, and she headed a group of women who were able to enlist help through their contacts and their wealth. Their efforts were indeed remarkable. There was a continuous struggle to fund the activities and to keep the facilities up to the task. Many material problems were solved by the financial contribution of individual Board members. Occasional events such as dress parades or garden parties would be organised for specific fund raising projects.

Alan wrote down some more of his recollections of conditions at the hospital when he started:

The buildings comprised the original main double-storied frontage from 1935 and additions to this including 2 consulting rooms, an operating theatre, cattery, kennels, waiting bays, pharmacy, Board room, and staff facilities. The original horse casting yard provided a delightful green area around which the buildings were grouped. Some remaining stables were used as storage areas. While most of these buildings were solidly built they were starting to appear dated and the more recent additions of cattery and kennels, because of heavy usage, were beginning to show signs of wear. So the impression was one of a rather old and tired but nevertheless substantial institution.

(Comments from the minutes in October 1960 give an insight into another aspect of the hospital conditions: 'Body and cat destruction room [is] constructed in fibro and corrugated iron, so [it is] impossible to keep cool' and in hot weather 'smells pervaded the whole area'.)

Basically two full-time and several part-time veterinary surgeons provided the veterinary services. They were assisted by veterinary nurses who were in many ways the corner-stone of the facility because they tended to stay longer. The vets rapidly gained the clinical expertise they deemed necessary to commence in outside practice and then moved on. There were less than thirty private practices in Melbourne at the start of the sixties, and, because the Lort Smith provided them with such a variety of clinical cases, they were soon able to gain enough experience to branch out on their own. Outstanding amongst the nurses was Simon Fraser. He had a huge depth of experience and gladly helped any new graduate without trespassing on their new found authority. Simon was in fact the mainstay of the hospital for many years acting as caretaker of the building and the inpatients when no vets were around. Nan Muller was a nurse who played a large part in lifting the standard of nursing during the 1960s. A capable woman, with a deep concern for the well-being of animals, she endeavoured to teach her fellow nurses the best ways to carry out any veterinary task.

The Veterinary Board of Victoria continued to disallow the spaying of animals as a way of protecting the livelihoods of private practitioners. This often meant that the animals of poorer people had numerous litters, and the Lort Smith had to deal with the resultant high numbers of animals requiring euthanasia. Milk fever and caesarean sections were also common.

The hospital finances were precarious. It was a week to week proposition and the tenacious dedication of the Board members must never be forgotten or underestimated.

At the beginning of 1960 three full-time vets were employed: Mr Capell, who resigned in April, Mr Pulvirenti (appointed January 1959) and Mr Tudhope. Mr Moreton was the secretary/manager until he retired from the position in April 1962 and Mrs Kretz was the matron. Richard Nemec particularly remembers that there was a close bond between Mr Tudhope and Simon Fraser because of their shared Scottish heritage.

Simon Fraser's twenty-five years of hospital service were celebrated on 2 May 1961 with an afternoon tea provided by the Board. He was presented with a silver salver signed by all members of the committee and Nell Fraser was given a bouquet of flowers. Nell later developed Alzheimer's disease, a cause of great distress to Simon, and she died on 2 February 1971. Simon Fraser retired as a veterinary nurse in 1970 but continued to live and work at the hospital in the role of caretaker until 1974 when he left the hospital to live with relatives in Bass. Simon died on 22 August 1980.

The year 1960 began with difficulties arising from a blurring of professional roles and boundaries. In February 1960 the matron, Mrs Kretz, was told by Dame Mabel in no uncertain terms that she was not to interfere in the veterinary work of the hospital. Later that month she was dismissed for continuing to meddle in the work of Mr Pulvirenti. Six staff members protested at her sacking, including the vet Mr Capell. They were all interviewed and reprimanded by Dame Mabel, no doubt for their audacity at questioning a Board decision.

Mrs Kretz was succeeded as matron by Rita Gower, who had several periods of prolonged absence due to sickness. There were indications in the minutes that Rita did not feel supported or respected by the staff, and she sometimes asked the Board for back-up over particular issues. For instance in March 1960 she reported dissatisfaction with the staff under her charge and the Board decided that Mr Moreton, the secretary/manager, should be authorised to terminate the employment of any of the present yard staff who failed to comply with her instructions, or who showed hostility to her authority. In October 1960 the Board sacked two staff members for refusing to obey her instructions.

In July 1961 a new vet, Mr McDonald, was appointed head vet although Mr Pulvirenti had been employed for longer. Mr McDonald was to attend Board meetings to advise on ethical and other problems affecting the smooth running of the hospital. He asked for access to the hospital's minutes and accounts to enable him to advise on the economic running of the practice, but this was an area over which the Board wished to retain its autonomy and the request was refused. Mr Watson, a friend of Mr McDonald, was appointed as a vet in January 1962.

The relationship between the head vet and the secretary/manager became untenable. In February 1962 Dame Mabel had to reprimand Mr McDonald for using force to try to prevent the secretary, Mr Moreton, passing through one of the surgeries. In spite of her telling the Board that there would be no repetition of such conduct there was further trouble. Unfortunately the details were not recorded but in early April Dame Mabel had interviews with the two vets, Mr Watson and Mr McDonald, and suspended them for forty-eight hours. More serious action against the two men was averted when they apologised to Mr Moreton. A letter to the Board from Mr Pulvirenti in March led to both Mr Watson and Mr McDonald being given six months' notice, but with the offer of reinstatement at a lower salary once their period of notice had expired. Mr Pulvirenti was given an immediate £200 increase. Unfortunately the contents of the letter were not recorded but it is likely to have been in relation to the incidents with the secretary/manager.

A further outcome of these events was the resignation of Mr Moreton who had already indicated in November 1961 that he was considering resigning as secretary/manager to take on the position of accountant at a lower rate of pay. At that time he was persuaded by the Board to remain in his existing position. When he formally tendered his resignation in March 1962 he was again asked not to leave until Dame Mabel returned from an overseas trip in August but after some consideration he replied that he would only remain as a part-time accountant. As he and the Board were unable to negotiate suitable terms he left the hospital almost immediately. Matron Rita Gower agreed to combine his duties with her own, and she appears to have quickly taken up the extra workload with the assistance of Mrs Phyllis (Phyl) Taylor.

There is no further record of Mr McDonald after the March incident. In June 1962 Mr Watson told the hospital that he wished to leave as soon as possible and Justin Barker was appointed on a temporary basis until Alan Lawther started on 30 October. In fact Justin Barker's temporary appointment was extended into 1963 when he turned down an offer of on-going work because he was not prepared to enter into a contract. He was replaced by Mr Tonuma, but continued to do locum work.

Mrs Phyllis Taylor and Mrs Helen Allchin, both administrative staff members, provided great stability and skill during this period. Phyl acted in a senior capacity on several occasions, and in June 1964 she was given an increase of £1 a week and a bonus of £25 'as a gesture of appreciation for the wonderful way she has carried the extra burden under difficult conditions'. Although she was offered a permanent position of secretary on several occasions she declined to accept it.

Since Phyl had never learnt to type she enlisted Helen's assistance on the Wednesday after each Board meeting to type the minutes and any letters required. Phyl remembers some anxious times when there was not enough money to pay the wages; a loan had to be arranged from a Board member or the solicitor, Mr Crowther.

Mrs Helen Allchin got to know the hospital well during the early 1950s through her involvement with the Cat Protection Society, and she became a volunteer with the Animal Welfare League. When the hospital was looking for people to staff its night service she was appointed as a receptionist/cashier for two nights a week for £1 10s per night. She started on 17 February 1959 and later became a hospital supervisor. She and Phyl Taylor worked well together as a team. Helen retired on 21 October 1975 after seventeen years but returned to work at the hospital when she was elected onto the committee on 17 March 1981. She worked tirelessly until she died on 16 January 1999.

Mrs Helen Allchin,
Photo: Lort Smith Animal Hospital.

In May 1961, exactly twelve months after the previous crisis, Mr Crowther again drew the attention of the Board to the critical financial situation. This was the third year in succession that the Board was surprised by the revelation of such bad financial news and it is hard to understand how such a state of affairs could have been allowed to develop.

Maybe the fact that they had 'got by' in the past provided little incentive for the Board to keep a tight rein on the financial situation, particularly since they were always able to cover their losses through alternative sources of revenue. In 1960 the amount raised by donations, subscriptions and fundraising reached £2919 while legacies amounted to £7500. The hospital deficit for 1960 was £8775, and this rose to £11,326 in 1961. A reply was drafted informing Mr Crowther that the Board would redouble its efforts to raise money, the president was to see the Premier of Victoria on 9 May to press for an increased government grant, and a public appeal was to be held in December 1961. The Board promised to 'keep the matter under close attention during the coming months'.

In November the financial situation was still precarious. The treasurer, Jack Smith, told the Board that the hospital could not continue at the present rate of expenditure and that severe cuts must be made. Mr Crowther reinforced the point, saying that it was the finance advisory committee's opinion that at the present rate of expenditure the hospital could not exist financially for longer than two years. And in the meantime, staffing problems persisted.

A new vet, Mr Neasey, was employed in December 1960. He accepted the position on condition that the League pay relocation expenses for his family, and that his accommodation be subsidised by £2 10s per week for thirteen weeks. He left after less than two months. In November Mr Tudhope gave notice of his resignation to take effect from 3 February 1961, but on 17 January 1961 he was informed by the Board that he would be paid to that date 'but he need not attend the hospital again'. He was replaced by Mr Lim, who started in March, but left in August.

In November Mr Pulvirenti's request for an increase in salary from £2000 to £3000 per annum was turned down. Not only was Mr Pulvirenti's request rejected, but the secretary was instructed to prepare suggestions for the finance advisory committee on closing the night service and having the hospital open for one eight-hour shift per day. On 5 December 1961 the decision was also made to close the pharmacy and to employ only one ambulance driver, but at the next meeting these decisions were deferred until the end of January 1962 on Dame Mabel's authorisation.

After a good deal of discussion, including a meeting between Dame Mabel and the finance committee, the Board took a completely new tack to try to resolve the deficit problem. The hospital would take in boarders. This decision was taken in February 1962 and Board member Mrs Adam agreed to discuss with an architect the expansion of the boarding facilities. An architect from the firm Leighton Irwin presented plans to a Board meeting in March, and estimated the cost to be between £1700 and £2000. No decision was made, and no further discussion of the plans ever took place. The major staffing disruptions around this time seem to have taken centre stage. In June 1962 Mr Pulvirenti was granted a salary of £3500, considerably more than he had requested and been refused only six months earlier.

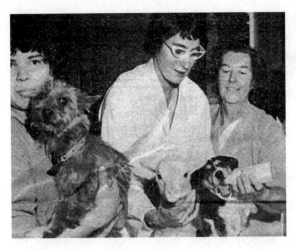

Miss Marianne Lucas nurses Shocko, Miss Jan Quintino holds Henry the lamb and Mrs Edna Otter feeds a lost pup, *Unidentified newspaper, AWL scrapbook.*

The Board's thinking appears to have reached a turning point around this time. Although the serious financial situation continued the annual deficits no longer assumed crisis proportions. The finance advisory committee gave up putting the same effort into alerting the Board when things were looking bad, perhaps recognising that this was a waste of its energies. The League managed to keep afloat as donations and legacies continued to arrive. The staffing situation improved.

After these turbulent couple of years the veterinary work of the hospital seems to have stabilised with the team of Joe Pulvirenti, Alan Lawther (started October 1962) and Mr Tonuma as the permanent vets. In mid-1963 an additional vet was employed on Wednesday and Thursday afternoons as the relieving vet, Mr Nemec, went overseas. A new vet was appointed, but the Board received negative feedback about his work and it was agreed that Justin Barker should be asked to return. Six months later Alan Lawther and Mr Tonuma told the Board that it was essential that two vets were always on duty because a single vet could not cope with the workload and the waiting list was intolerable. Consequently another vet was taken on.

In March 1964 Jan Quintino was appointed and trained as a veterinary assistant. She worked for nine years at the hospital and after she resigned she was invited to join the Board. Alan Lawther thought highly of her knowledge and skills.

Vets continued to be very hard to attract, and in May 1967 an English vet, Miss Kenyon, was sponsored to work at the hospital which facilitated her assisted passage from the UK. Mrs Allchin provided her with accommodation on her arrival and she was allowed to do a short course at the Werribee Veterinary Clinic to gain additional skills. She resigned in May 1969.

Dr Nemec continued to do locum work at the hospital after his return but resigned because of ill health in mid 1965. Mr Tonuma also resigned in 1965. Don Tynan, who had started as a locum in April 1965, later worked full-time for the hospital, and then ran the night clinic.

In January 1966 Dr Alan Lawther had asked for a reduction of hours worked. A decision was deferred but was agreed to when he threatened to resign. In July 1967 he again told the Board that he wished to resign, but after some reassessment he changed his mind. On behalf of the hospital, he had had to accept a good deal of criticism from vets in private practice, and he told the Board about some of his concerns including the underhand practices of some vets who encouraged the staff to refer animals to them privately. In October 1968 Alan resigned to set up his own clinic in Templestowe, but within a month, due to a shortage of staff, he had accepted a request to return for one day a week to perform operations. This later increased to one-and-a-half days but for a while there was an arrangement whereby animals were sent by ambulance to Dr Lawther's clinic for operations to be performed there.

Phyl Taylor describes Alan as having been one of the best veterinary surgeons in Melbourne, and very good with his hands. This was recognised by the veterinary profession and he used to perform 'cutting edge' surgery at the Victorian Veterinary Institute when other surgeons would watch him in action. Because the operating theatre was in such an enclosed space the operation was shown on a closed-circuit television to an audience in another room. On one occasion he and veterinary nurse Nan Muller were operating on a dog's ear when the dog died under the anaesthetic. Neither gave any indication of the death but continued to perform the operation as though it were still living. He was later congratulated on his skill in controlling the dog's bleeding.

In February 1968 Dr Pulvirenti resigned after nine years because of the pressure of work in his own practice. In 1969 Dr Joan Humphreys joined the staff. She resigned in March 1972 but continued to do locum work at the hospital, and in particular to spay cats. In December 1968 the Board agreed that a new member of staff was needed to eliminate excess overtime by other staff members who were becoming tired.

After the resignation of Mr Pulvirenti there does not appear to have been any vet with any length of experience or who took any particular initiative. Vets came and went. It was also difficult to obtain administrative staff because higher wages were being paid elsewhere for less demanding work. In February 1973, to attract suitable staff and to compensate for the nature of the work, the secretary was authorised to offer a $2 per week increase to full-time female employees and $3 to ambulance drivers.

Among the vets who worked at this time was Dr Gerry Clarkson who was employed part-time from 1966 to 1968, and again for a short time in 1972 as a locum.

Rita Gower continued to have trouble with the staff in her role of secretary/manager. In April 1963 she reported that, contrary to hospital policy, strays were being destroyed without her knowledge, and that she would appreciate the Board's support in gaining the co-operation of the vets regarding stray animals. In November 1963 she said that the crematorium was to be completed soon and she requested that the Board issue an order to all staff members 'that her instructions regarding use of said crematorium be followed implicitly'. She resigned in June 1964 and was replaced by Miss Kaye, who in turn resigned in March 1965 due to sudden ill health. Phyl Taylor was again reluctant to take on the role of secretary/manager but filled in until April when Mrs Stanleigh was appointed on a trial basis. She was not well fitted for the job and was asked to leave when her three-month probationary period finished. The Board asked Phyl to give Mrs Stanleigh the news – in her own words, the Board members did not like to get their hands dirty – and she felt quite intimidated. She asked her friend Helen Allchin to be present for support, but hidden in a small alcove known as the vault.

Dr Cimati outside his residence,
Photo: Graham Cornish.

At last Phyl agreed to take on the position permanently, and she stayed for nine years. In December 1974 she resigned on medical advice, only to return yet again in April 1976 when her replacement, Maureen Gallop, resigned. When the Board proposed that Phyl should receive the same salary as Mrs Gallop she volunteered to accept $20 a week less 'which she felt was at the moment adequate'. She finally resigned in 1978, but even after that she did occasionally fill in for staff absences into the 1990s.

In 1978 Mrs Kwiatek was appointed to the position of secretary/manager, a position she held until 1987. She was an outstanding accountant, very exact, and is described by Board member David White as one of the top half dozen accountants he has ever dealt with. She had previously worked in a hospital and her experience of working in a hierarchical setting made her an excellent secretary/manager, able to cooperate well with the veterinary staff, and she had a particularly good relationship with Dr Cimati.

Dr Cimati was appointed in May 1974 at a salary of $8000. In November, with his wife and two children, he moved into the newly painted flat above the hospital, recently vacated by Simon Fraser. In February 1975 he was appointed senior veterinary surgeon with responsibility for the employment and direction of the vets. It was envisaged that this would take some of the load off the newly appointed secretary, Maureen Gallop, and generally be to the benefit of the hospital and for this he was given an increase in salary. In May his salary was raised yet again because of his emergency night work. As many of the clients he was seeing at night were not genuine emergencies he was provided with a phone to check whether a case required immediate treatment.

Dr Cimati remembers that conditions at the hospital at that time were appalling. Water used to drain off the roof and blow across the floor of the operating theatre onto the concrete outside because of the way the door was constructed. There was also a concrete drain running under the floor of the theatre covered only by a plank of wood. This was not only unhygienic but, according to Alan Lawther, smelt very nasty.

It was not only the physical conditions that were bad; the relationships between the staff were ruled by factions and often vets would not speak to each other. This led to some very unprofessional practice. No vet ever stayed very long, but with the appointment of new staff Dr Cimati was eventually able to bring about something of a change of culture.

In 1975 Dr Ben David was appointed, and when he left in August 1977 he was not immediately replaced, leaving Dr Cimati to work a seven day week. In April 1979 Dr Cimati was appointed to the sub-committee which was formed to plan and oversee the hospital renovations. In May 1979 the Board recognised his value to the hospital by paying for him to attend a veterinary conference in Moscow.

In June 1976 a decision was made which was to have significant implications for the organisation of the hospital finances. The original articles of association severely restricted what investments the League could make, and with rising interest rates and the possibility of making capital gains through investing in property or the stock market it was decided, on advice obtained through Sadie Howe, who had replaced Dame Mabel as president, that the situation should be reviewed. The articles of association were changed at an emergency meeting, with the permission of the Attorney-General, to allow the League to invest more widely and deal in shares, fixed interest or property. According to Phyl Taylor, who was the hospital secretary at that time, this was a very significant event and allowed the League far greater control over its financial destiny. She and John Honey, the current finance manager, believe that Sadie Howe was a very astute businesswoman. Sadie was to play a large part in deciding the investment strategies of the League for a good many years.

Year	Deficit	Accumulated funds	Net current assets
1960	$18,000 (£8775)	$9200 (£4602)	$145,000 (£72,424)
1979	$165,880	$159,015	$53,465

A review of the hospital's finances in 1979 showed that the deficit had increased almost ten-fold over the previous two decades. But whereas the net current assets had decreased by approximately one-third, the accumulated funds had increased significantly due to generous fundraising, donations and bequests and the changes in investment policy. It was against this financial scenario that the Board had to make its next major decision – whether or not to undertake substantial renovations.

During the 1970s there was a good deal of community disquiet about the funding of animal welfare, and in particular the situation at the Lost Dogs' Home where the Lethanair machine was being used to euthanase dogs because of the high cost of lethal injections. According to Dr Cimati, it was extensive political lobbying by influential women such as the committee members of the Animal Welfare League which encouraged a shaky Liberal government under Mr Rupert Hamer to consider giving funding to the animal welfare cause.

In February 1979 the Lost Dogs' Home indicated that it wanted to operate a twenty-four hour service and was seeking government funding – further competition for scarce resources. The Board decided to take a proactive approach, and Mrs Howe was delegated to visit Mr Hamer, the Victorian Premier, to explain that the Lort Smith was already operating a hospital in the area which, with further aid, could provide a twenty-four hour service.

Sadie Howe, David White and Mrs Kwiatek met Mr Hamer on 22 March 1979. They were given positive news – both the Lort Smith Hospital and the Lost Dogs' Home were to be given financial help on the basis of a two-for-one grant to update their facilities. There was concern that the hospital might not be able to afford to accept a two-for-one condition because of its limited financial resources. The possibility of holding an appeal was considered but deferred as one had already been started by the Lost Dogs' Home. It was a 'once in a lifetime' opportunity, and the League decided to accept the grant and the financial risks associated with it.

The hospital had occupied the same building for forty-four years. Many areas needed to be updated. A sub-committee was formed to plan and oversee the work: Sadie Howe, Alan Lawther, David White, Joyce Quintino and Dr Cimati.

Keeping up to date: 1980-1990

The Board and the administrative staff remained remarkably stable throughout the 1980s. There were only two secretary/managers, and all the new appointments to the Board had a close association with the hospital, either by having been a staff member or having a close relationship with another Board member. Alan Lawther left the Board around 1984 but returned in the early 1990s when he was appointed managing director. Dr Joan Humphreys, who had worked as a vet at the hospital, also joined the Board for a short period in June 1986 but, according to Alan Lawther, she became very frustrated at the decision-making processes and left after only three months.

Three people who had already made a significant contribution to the hospital were elected to the Board in 1981: Mrs Phyllis Taylor, who had resigned as hospital secretary in 1978; Mrs Helen Allchin, who had resigned in December 1975 after having been a member of staff for twenty-one years; and Mr David Alsop, an architect with the firm of Garnet Alsop and partners which had been employed to plan and supervise the new building. This firm had been selected because of their experience in building for animals, having been involved with the building of Melbourne University's Veterinary school at Werribee, Healesville Sanctuary and the Melbourne Zoo.

Mrs Pat Patience also joined the Board in 1981. Her association with the League had started in 1952 when she joined Mrs Lort Smith in supporting the anti-cruelty campaign and she had assisted by writing the minutes of the meetings.

The 1980s were both challenging and satisfying years for the Board. On the one hand, inflation was high, and staff continued to cause management problems. On the other hand, during the first years of the decade the government was very generous to animal welfare, allowing the hospital to undergo some substantial improvements – but these were demanding of the Board's time. In order to take full advantage of the government's two-for-one grant the hospital had to ensure that it had sufficient funds to meet its own commitments. One thing in the Board's favour was that interest rates were high and they were able to capitalise on their prudent investments.

Mrs Virginia Edwards, Mrs Jane Alsop, Mrs Vena Davey, Mrs Helen Allchin, Mr David Alsop, Mrs Elizabeth Osborne, Lady Murray, Mrs Sadie Howe, Mrs Sheila White, Mrs Phyl Taylor and Mrs Pat Patience, October 1984. Gloves were worn on this occasion by order of Government House, *Photo: Graham Cornish.*

The Board continued to receive the support of professionals who gave their advice on a voluntary basis. The firm Weigall and Crowther had been very generous in discounting its legal advice to the hospital and an example was the firm's bill for advice given in relation to the Veterinary Board in October 1982: the amount of $525 was reduced to $325. In August 1983 Mr Crowther told the Board that he would continue to be available to give his personal advice to the League on an honorary basis on any matters within his province but that all other services would be billed to the League at the firm's actual cost.

At the end of the 1980s there was one issue over which the Board fought a particularly vicious battle. Within living memory Board meetings had always been held at 2 pm, but with more members in business this time was becoming increasing unsuitable. Mr Osborne, who had joined in 1966, was an example of those who opposed any change. He said that he would not attend evening meetings because of transport congestion, parking problems and the cold. Mrs Patience said that an evening time would disrupt her family life. Mrs Edwards and Mr Alsop preferred the evening slot because of their business commitments. Alternating times were trialled, followed by a vote on 5 September 1989 which came down in favour of the 2 pm time by seven votes to four with Mrs Howe, the Chair, abstaining. She commented that she was distressed that the matter had served to split the Board for the first time in her long association with the hospital.

This was not to be the end of the debate. A short time later Mr Alsop suggested a 1 pm meeting time with a light lunch provided to allow business people to return to work when the meeting had finished. After more discussion this was finally agreed to, with the proviso that specific agenda items requiring particular attention be brought forward to allow people needing to return to work to leave early.

Sadie Howe resigned as chairperson soon after this issue had been resolved, and on 17 October 1989 Mr Ian Dodd, who had been elected to the Board in October 1988, was elected as the new chairman.

Two incidents during 1989 demonstrate how the hospital was changing:

- When, in April 1989, the hospital administration thought fit to terminate a staff member's service for alleged rudeness, the staff argued on her behalf and she was offered reinstatement – hardly an approach that Dame Mabel would have sanctioned. It demonstrated the extent to which the rigid autocratic control that had characterised staff management in the early years had eased. A requirement of reinstatement was that the staff member appear before the Board to be told that a change in attitude was required in future contact with the public.
- In August Ian Davey offered to donate a computer to the hospital, its first. It was able to record and read the silicon implant information used to identify animals and it was used to deal with some of the hospital's administrative functions. One of Ian's friends, Peter Louis, also generously donated his time to install the software.

Despite careful monitoring and prudent management the hospital continued to run at a deficit. Inflation, particularly during the 1980s, led to many close examinations as to how money could be saved without cutting essential and profitable services.

Audited accounts for 1981 showed an operating loss of $252,420. In April 1982 the award rate for veterinary assistants rose by $20 a week, and it was agreed that vets should be paid an increase of $1250 a year. Bad debts continued to be a problem – $403.50 was written off in June 1982, an unusually high amount, but an indication of how seriously clients' failure to pay could impact on the service. Frequently bad debts occurred because clients had given a false address. The introduction of the use of Bankcard in August 1983 was an attempt to address this.

Several bequests to the League included property. Houses and flats which could be rented without a great deal of maintenance were often leased, sometimes to people who found it difficult to lease premises on the private market because they owned pets. Rent proved a useful income stream to the hospital. And of course fundraising remained another major source of revenue.

A new crematorium was the first priority for spending the government grant as the old one had proved very unreliable over the last few years. According to Dr Cimati, the burning process was very unsatisfactory: fat from the cremated dogs used to run under the door and trickle down the yard outside the waiting bays (at this time situated on the south side of the hospital) to ooze down the gutters in Villiers Street. When the firing did not go well, so much smoke from the burner used to drift into the waiting bays that it was difficult to see through the haze. These conditions were hardly encouraging for clients waiting with would-be patients.

Many visits were made to different establishments to research the best kind of crematorium to purchase. The installation went ahead without major difficulties, although problems were reported in the early stages of its use.

Work continued with the building of two operating theatres, a reception area and new waiting rooms. The hot water, heating and other mechanical services were also upgraded. New equipment included operating lights, theatre tables, an anaesthetic machine, trolleys, waiting room chairs and a computerised cash register. Initially the state government agreed to grant the hospital $120,000, but this was increased in February 1981 to $170,000.

A further state government grant of up to $133,000, on the same two-for-one basis and announced in November 1982, facilitated the reconstruction of the kennel area. It was immediately suggested that as much information as possible be obtained about the design of kennels, particularly from America. There was a frustrating delay in obtaining building permits because the Melbourne City Council had difficulty categorising the hospital under its regulations. The tender was finally accepted in March 1983 for $191,462. The first stage of the building, which comprised the new kennel complex and included an isolation section and a larger modernised laundry, was complicated by the discovery of some buried concrete beams under the old stables which had to be removed. The ground was swampy and an additional five-and-a-half feet (about two metres) of soil had to be excavated to allow for laying foundations. This stage was completed during 1983. The next stage, the renovation of the kennel area, was completed soon after and included two dog wards, an intensive care ward, a new kitchen to prepare animals' meals and new dog runs. In 1982 the administration area was repainted, the old red and black floor tiles were replaced to improve safety standards and studded rubber flooring was placed on the ramp up to the cat wards and on two smaller ramps in the administration area.

Old kennels were replaced in 1983,
Photo: Graham Cornish.

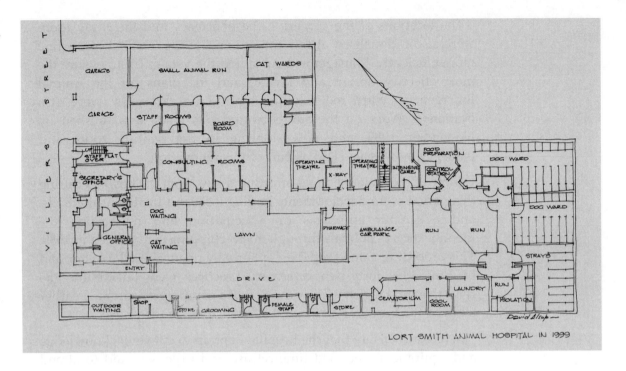

Inside the floor plan (labels):

STREET

GARAGE SMALL ANIMAL RUN CAT WARDS

GARAGE STAFF ROOMS BOARD ROOM

VILLIER STREET

STAFF FLAT OVER CONSULTING ROOMS OPERATING THEATRE OPERATING THEATRE INTENSIVE CARE CONTROL STATION FOOD PREPARATION DOG WARD

SECRETARY'S OFFICE X-RAY

DOG WAITING LAWN PHARMACY AMBULANCE CAR PARK RUN RUN DOG WARD

GENERAL OFFICE CAT WAITING STRAYS

ENTRY DRIVE LAUNDRY RUN ISOLATION

OUTDOOR WAITING SHOP STORE GROOMING FEMALE STAFF STORE CREMATORIUM COOL ROOM

David Alsop —

LORT SMITH ANIMAL HOSPITAL IN 1999

The League was fortunate that several substantial grants were made by the Scobie and Claire Mackinnon Trust, the first, $2500, in July 1982. Three further cheques, each for $5000 were received over the next three years. These would have been particularly welcome because the hospital had lost revenue due to the disruption caused by the rebuilding.

Lady Murray, the hospital's patron, officially opened the renovated hospital on 11 October 1984. Two hundred guests attended, and a marquee was erected over the exercise lawn.

The process of refurbishing and updating the hospital continued. X-ray facilities were improved and a grooming room for stray dogs was planned. More movable canvas blinds were provided for the exercise yards. In 1986 a two-way radio system was installed with a base station to allow communication with the three hospital ambulances. A new anaesthetic machine was purchased with money donated to the hospital, and some new surgical equipment was acquired to bring the hospital up to date. In 1988 the cattery was refurbished.

Layout of the hospital after reconstructions,
Graphics: David Alsop.

The locations of the surgeries, the pharmacy and the X-ray room were also rationalised at this time to enable the hospital to operate more efficiently. Management consulted the vets to try to ensure the most effective design and layout, and the plans for the Animal Emergency Centre redevelopment at Mount Waverley were also examined. Work on the surgeries and pharmacy was finished by November 1989, and new flooring in the waiting room and passageway was also laid as part of this renovation.

Some of the major changes affecting the work of the hospital during this period were developments in diagnosis and treatment methods, and a greater emphasis on vaccination and neutering. The identification of animals through micro-chipping commenced in 1989. This procedure gained rapid acceptance by many animal owners, and by June 1989 forty-two veterinary practices were linked into the central animal registry. The donation of a computer mentioned earlier allowed the Lort Smith Hospital to participate in the project.

In order to ensure that the hospital kept up to date in its knowledge and equipment, vets had time release and expenses paid to attend seminars and conferences. Some of the topics included acupuncture, dental care of animals and neurological disorders in cats and dogs. The vets were expected to report back to the Board and to their colleagues.

In August 1988 the Board confirmed its policy regarding the neutering of animals which up to then had changed frequently. All animals had to be neutered before they were sold unless they were too young, in which case the owner had to sign a document agreeing to return the animal for neutering at the appropriate time. Where pedigrees were available these were not to be given to the new owner until neutering was completed. This policy remains unchanged and is in line with current legislative requirements and codes of practice.

In 1980 the improved facilities enabled the hospital to cope with a greater workload, and 42,182 animals were treated, of which 6577 were strays. The number of stray dogs was 1845, of which 260 were claimed and 529 were found new homes. Homes were found for 820 of the 4732 stray cats. It was a particularly busy year because of an outbreak of parvovirus which meant that many owners brought their dogs in either for vaccination or for treatment: the number of patients exceeded 100 every day. The problem was compounded by the fact that the vaccine was unavailable for several months.

On 7 May 1984 Dr Cimati told the Board that the hospital had had the busiest April ever, and the following month he said that the previous year had been the busiest in the history of the hospital, as the updated facilities were used to the full. The number of animals treated was 47,630, an increase of more than 5000 over the 1980 number, and homes were found for 916 dogs (529 in 1980) and 1464 cats (820 in 1980). The number of vets was increased to ten to meet the extra demand. In November 1985 a night service was reintroduced, with a vet and a nurse available from 8.30 pm to midnight seven days a week to cope with animals requiring emergency treatment. Dr Cimati, Dr Fattohi and Dr Kilpatrick covered the night service.

The hospital continued to invest in new equipment as it became available. In 1988 it introduced a blood centrifuge and a blood biochemistry analyser which would enable tests that were being performed at a laboratory at Blackburn to be carried out on the premises. This saved a wait of between twelve and forty-eight hours since results of tests done on the premises could be obtained within fifteen to thirty minutes. An additional benefit was that nursing staff were able to operate the equipment thus considerably reducing the cost.

In September 1989 Dr Sequeira reported to the Board that the hospital was performing surgical procedures on a regular basis which were previously only possible at specialist clinics. This was particularly the case with orthopaedic surgery. He also reported that the hospital's pathology unit coped with all everyday needs and it was only necessary to have some specialised tests and autopsy cases performed by outside units.

Staffing appears to have stabilised by the mid 1980s. June Price was appointed to the administrative staff in 1983, and she remained until 1995. When she started there were only five people in the office, and they were under the stern and watchful eye of Mrs Kwiatek. June remembers that conditions in those days were tough. When anybody was sick staff were expected to cover without any negotiation, and similarly if someone was not available for a night shift it was taken for granted that one of the day staff would fill in. There was no rigid demarcation of work-staff had to cover lunch and tea breaks, so everyone was multi-skilled. The only exception was Mrs Kwiatek. One day, June remembers, Mrs Kwiatek arrived late for work, an almost unheard-of event. A staff member, afraid that Mrs Kwiatek would not be on time for the opening of the hospital, took the cash boxes from the safe. When Mrs Kwiatek arrived she almost exploded with rage – that was one duty most definitely her own. Another closely guarded job was the typing of the Board minutes, which fell to June. She had to do this on a rickety old machine, and observe the greatest secrecy. Her desk was situated in a very public position so she had to cover the typewriter whenever anyone walked past.

June recalls that staff selection was a very secret process, and she was briefed before she attended for her interview that she was to wait outside until Mrs Kwiatek arrived to let her in through the front door rather than the normal side entrance. She was ushered out quickly by the same door so she would not be observed by the staff. The explanation: 'They all talk!' June was not the preferred candidate for the job because she had no experience in working with animals, but the person who was first offered the job turned it down because she was not given a parking space. It was four years before June finally graduated to having her parking space allotted in the garage.

Although Mrs Kwiatek was a demanding boss she was very protective of her team and would stand up for them if there were any arguments with the veterinary staff. There was frequent conflict with the vets, and this was often because the administrative staff were the 'meat in the sandwich' between the clients, frustrated and uncomfortable because of the long time they had to wait, and the overworked vets. Attempts were made at different times to improve the system of seeing clients. For instance one vet seeing simple cases – such as an animal requiring removal of stitches or vaccinations – was tried but this did not work well because clients would try to prolong the consultation by bringing up other issues, and waiting clients could not understand why some apparently well animals were seen before their more sickly ones.

In April 1982 the paymaster and bookkeeper, Mr R. Davidson, was seriously injured in a rail crossing accident in which his wife died. He retired in July, and was replaced in August by Mr John Honey, the present day finance manager.

In 1980 there were five vets: Dr Cimati (senior vet), Dr Jan Fattohi (started in September), Dr Rod Brooks, Dr Trevor Davey and Dr Caroline Letts. Dr Joan Humphreys had also returned to work in the hospital two days a week, mainly spaying animals. Dr Andrew Cameron commenced in December 1980. Dr Letts left in January 1981.

The high turnover of junior veterinary staff at the hospital continued, but the effect was ameliorated by the relative stability of the senior staff. Nevertheless the junior vets did give cause for concern and there were times when the Board acknowledged that there were lapses in the standard of the service provided. In February 1987 the Board received a report that one of the vets had been accepting payment for treating animals owned by members of the staff in hospital time and on hospital premises. The vet, who had been employed on and off for ten years, was given one week's pay in lieu of notice. Another vet who had been appointed in 1984 had his services terminated in 1987 due to insolence, and his refusal to share the services of a nurse and to see clients when his rostered nurse was away due to illness.

In November 1982 it was suggested that the vets be issued with two-year contracts 'to make them work harder'. The minutes for that November meeting also reported Dr Lawther as saying that the standard of veterinary care provided by the nurses was slipping. Only twelve of the forty-eight graduates of that year's TAFE course for veterinary nurses had been successful in gaining positions, so it was envisaged that there would be no difficulty in recruiting new staff. A new award had added over $15 a week per employee to salary costs – and this was on top of the $20 a week increase granted at the start of the year. In order to save money on wages paid to veterinary nurses it was suggested (but not implemented) that shifts be cut from twelve to eight hours and the hospital close at 8 pm instead of 9 pm so that the hospital would not have to pay overtime rates. According to their award, no overtime was paid to veterinary nurses for weekday work, or work performed before 12.30 pm on Saturday, provided only eight hours were worked. Any shift which finished after 8 pm attracted a 15% penalty for the whole shift. Incidentally the veterinary surgeons were not covered by an award until the late 1990s.

In April 1984 the vets were being provided with regular salary increases of $500 every six months and the retention rate had increased – they were now staying for more than three years. In December 1984 the Board unanimously agreed that the vets' salaries were too low and Dr Cimati's salary was raised to $25,000, and the rest of the vets received an increase of $1000 per annum.

Dr Cimati resigned in April 1985 to take effect from 2 June but, because it was difficult to replace him, he continued his work at the hospital for two more years on a part-time basis. When Dr Cimati left his flat above the hospital Dr Kilpatrick and his wife, Dr Blackie, moved in. The vets were unsettled by not having a senior vet on the premises, and various concerns were expressed that the vets were not working together, as well as about the standard of practice. Attempts

Dr Fattohi and Mrs Myrna Mclaughlan, a hospital volunteer, 1980's, *Photo: Lort Smith Animal Hospital.*

Staff members Mrs Chris Farrell and Mrs Marion Adcock, *Photo: Lort Smith Animal Hospital.*

Veterinary staff: Dr Cimati, Dr Kilpatrick, Dr Botterill, Dr Alan Sultan, Dr Rita Geroe, 1984, *Photo: Lort Smith Animal Hospital.*

to find a suitable senior vet from outside the hospital were not successful so Dr Jan Fattohi, who had joined the hospital in 1980, was promoted to the position in 1987 on the recommendation of Dr Cimati. Dr Fattohi left in August 1988 and was in turn replaced by Dr José Sequeira, with Dr Kilpatrick acting in that capacity at weekends until he left in September of that year.

Dr José Sequeira was appointed in 1982. Born in East Timor, he had graduated in Portugal where he worked for two years before migrating to Australia. Dr Euan Kilpatrick started in February 1982 and Dr Heather Blackie joined the staff in 1984. When Euan Kilpatrick left the hospital to set up in private practice in Frankston the flat which he had occupied was rented by Tom and Chris Farrell. Tom Farrell was a security guard so was considered by the Board to be a most suitable tenant. Tom and Chris continue to live in the flat fourteen years later, and Chris is a member of the hospital staff.

Vladimir Kogan was appointed to the staff in April 1981. He had been a veterinary surgeon in his home country, Soviet Russia, but had left as a political refugee in 1977 and had spent nine months in Italy before being given clearance to enter Australia. He tried for about three years to have his qualifications and experience recognised by the Veterinary Board in Australia. Despite a visit by a veterinary science professor from South Australia to Moscow and St Petersburg to check out the universities in which Vladimir had trained, with a positive report resulting from his trip, more bureaucratic red tape required that he sit exams. Finally Vladimir's health began to suffer and further study became unrealistic.

He worked for two and a half years on a project run by Dr Colin Wilks, now a professor at the Victorian Research Institute, on the disease leptospirosis. When the project came to an end and there was no funding for further research, Dr Cimati suggested that Vladimir take a job as a veterinary nurse at the Lort Smith Hospital and this was arranged with Mrs Kwiatek. He found it a little hard at first because, although a vet of many years' experience, he was used to working with large animals and chickens and had had little experience with cats and dogs. As a person with veterinary training and experience he was expected to have more knowledge than he in fact had, and he said that the first few months were a learning process both for him and for his colleagues. He recollects a golden labrador being brought in for treatment which, the owner had told him, was very friendly and never bit. But the dog did not take kindly to being restrained on a hospital table, with the result that Vladimir required six stitches in one finger and three weeks off work. Their stitches came out around the same time, and when the dog was brought back Vladimir again asked the owner if his dog was friendly. The owner reassured him that it was; then Vladimir showed him his wound: the dog growled at him again as if to prove a point!

Vladimir remembers that these were very busy years. The staff worked long hours – twelve-hour shifts were usual, and lunch breaks were staggered so that the maximum number of patients could be seen. Before the era of computers there was invariably a stack of cards for people waiting with their pets, and each was allocated to one of the three consulting rooms as a vet became available. The vets alternated between surgery and consulting and it was hard to fit in a suitable lunch break.

Vladimir worked closely as a veterinary nurse with Dr Andrew Cameron and later with Dr José Sequeira. He continued in this role until he severely injured his back lifting a large dog onto the theatre table. As he was unable to lift heavy loads after this, Mr Joyce, the secretary/manager who had replaced Mrs Kwiatek, suggested that he work in the pharmacy. For some time there had been no pharmacist, the load being shared between three veterinary nurses who rotated their other duties and the appointment of Vladimir as part-time pharmacist allowed them to concentrate on their nursing duties.

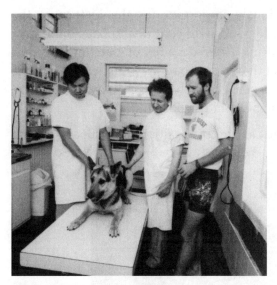

Dr José Sequeira and Mr Vladimir Kogan with patient and owner, *Photo: Graham Cornish.*

The nineties: preparing for a new millennium

The nineties were tremendously important for the history of the hospital. Decisions were made which will continue to have an impact for many years into the future. After decades of patching up and making do, it became evident that major changes were necessary if the hospital was to grow and prosper. These changes demanded courage, determination and commitment from the Board.

There had been few changes to the composition of the Board during the previous decade.

Board members Mrs Helen Allchin and Mrs Phyl Taylor with Mrs Joan Sturzaker (centre) enjoy a hospital function, *Photo: Lort Smith Animal Hospital.*

Mrs Pat Patience was elected vice-president in August 1991. Mr Don Osborne's death, in August 1992, followed by the resignation of his wife Elizabeth shortly afterwards, caused the committee to take stock of its composition. It was realised that several members were suffering from ill health and others were unable to attend meetings on a regular basis. There was a need to attract new members. The first to join was Susi Edwards, Virginia Edwards' cousin and also a granddaughter of inaugural vice-president Lady Vivien Clapp. Their grandfather, Sir Harold Clapp, had also played a part in animal welfare. As Commissioner for Railways he had been responsible in 1935 for bringing in specially designed ramps for safely unloading livestock from trains.

Susie Palmer had gained broad experience of the League, having served for two years as secretary, and she was elected to the Board in 1995.

Sadly, David White's wife Sheila, who had been a Board member since 1981, died in October 1998. In August 1998 Dr Gerry Clarkson was elected to the Board. He had worked at the hospital on a part-time basis from 1966 to 1968 while he completed his master's degree at the Veterinary School in 'Haematology and Serum Iron in the Racehorse'. He had lived across the road at the Redback Hotel, then called the Royal Hotel, on the corner of Villiers Street and Flemington Road. One of his closest neighbours was Simon Fraser with whom he became very friendly and thus established an interest in the early history of the hospital. Dr Clarkson travelled overseas after finishing his degree but returned to work as a locum in August 1972. He developed his own private practice in Box Hill in 1973 but later returned to study and completed two theses, one on women and the veterinary profession and the other on Harold Albiston, a pioneer of veterinary science in Victoria and one of the early vets who, through his involvement with the Australian Veterinary Association, had a minor role in the development of the Lort Smith Animal Hospital.

As a new hospital building was about to get under way, the appointment of a person with architectural skills on the Board was highly desirable. David Alsop had recently resigned because his son had contracted leukemia. Rick Macdonald was an architect whose firm had tendered unsuccessfully for the redevelopment of the hospital building. When Alan Lawther observed him looking at some stray dogs at the hospital he immediately recognised a compassionate animal lover from the way in which he handled and addressed the animals. Alan persuaded him to become involved in the management of the hospital in 1998. Maggie Allmand was employed in the pharmaceutical industry in the sales and marketing area. She joined the Board in June of the same year. Virginia Edwards suggested in 1999 that Samantha Baillieu be invited to become a member, but she

Mrs John Baillieu in 1938, *Unidentified newspaper, AWL scrapbook.*

DOG day ... Dr Sequeira treats a puppy. Picture: LISA BIGELOW

Animal aid wins award

MORE than 60 years of looking after dogs, cats and other beasts finally has been rewarded for the Lort Smith Animal Welfare Hospital.

The hospital, in North Melbourne, was one of 14 Victorian individuals and groups who yesterday received Advance Australia Awards for services to the community. Other award recipients were Olympic cyclist Kathy Watt, singer Marina Prior, racing car driver Mark Skaife and the Scienceworks Museum in Spotswood.

The hospital's senior veterinarian, Dr Jose Sequeira, said the award was a great honor to staff.

"We feel very proud to have our work recognised because we always try to do our best and there is a lot of stress involved," he said.

"The award makes us feel as though we are doing something good."

The hospital, funded partly by the Animal Welfare League, treats about 150 animals a day ranging from vaccinations to emergencies.

"Our charter says that we can't turn away from treating an animal and we have 12 fully qualified vets working every day," Dr Sequeira said.

CARE Australia worker Mary-Jane Hammond also received an award for her contribution to humanitarian care in the famine-struck areas of Somalia.

Ms Hammond was one of the first Australians to start emergency relief programs in Baidoa, one of the worst hit towns in Somalia, last year.

— KATE WILSON

Dr José Sequeira, *Herald Sun* 20 February 1993.

was badly injured in a riding accident and was not well enough to join until 2001. Members of the Baillieu family had been involved in the early history of the hospital and Samantha's mother-in-law, Mrs Elizabeth (John) Baillieu, had been an active fundraiser during the 1930s and served on the Board in the 1940s. (Mrs M. H. Baillieu had also been elected to the Board in June 1940 but did not attend a single meeting.)

Sadie Howe was given the honorary title of President Emeritus at the 1998 annual general meeting in recognition of her many years of service to the Animal Welfare League.

In 1992 the Lort Smith Hospital was nominated for an Advance Australia Award for outstanding contributions in the field of animal welfare. The Governor, the Honorable Richard McGarvie, presented the award at Government House on 19 February 1993 and Ian Dodd, Sadie Howe, Pat Patience and Dr José Sequeira attended.

The Board was excited to learn in June 1991 that the League's very first ambulance had been found on a property at Red Hill on the Mornington Peninsula. It had been bought by Mr Russell Stapleton who lived in Bright and whose hobby was the restoration of old commercial vehicles. His friend and partner, Richard Unkles, who later bought the ambulance, brought a photograph of it to the hospital. It was in a dilapidated condition, and he said that when it was restored it would be made available for hospital publicity. In return the committee agreed to pay for the sign-writing. In March 1993 the hospital, through David Alsop, expressed an interest in buying the ambulance; it was agreed that if it were for sale the League would have the first option to purchase for 85% of three independent valuations. In the meantime Ian Dodd and David Alsop, both old car enthusiasts, agreed to give all the assistance they could to ensure a faithful restoration of the vehicle. An old photograph was lent to them

Mr Richard Unkles shown with the partly restored original ambulance, 2000, *Photo: Keith Bedford.*

to help with details, and Marge Wreford, who had driven the ambulance in the 1930s, was taken to see it and asked for her recollections.

As the Board was becoming more involved in planning for the hospital's future it developed an increasing interest in its past. When Gerry Clarkson was appointed to the Board he agreed to coordinate the researching and writing of the history of the hospital. He had proven skills in this area, with his two previous historical theses. The project was entered into with great enthusiasm. Several interviews were conducted with past members of staff and volunteers. In August 1999 Gerry travelled to Canberra where he interviewed the hospital's first veterinary surgeon Ronald Greville, and his wife Nan, both of whom have since died. Joan Sturzaker and Virginia Edwards also interviewed past employees and volunteers. However, the project was vast and time was limited. It was finally agreed that the Board come to an arrangement with a person who would be paid to complete the history.

The hospital continued to trade at a deficit throughout the 1990s, while prices rose regularly in an attempt to increase the revenue. The question persisted of what was to be done with animals when the owner would not or could not pay their account, while the policy was reiterated that all animals were to be treated regardless of payment issues. In October 1990 the amount of unpaid debts for the previous two months totalled nearly $6000.

In the early 1990s the Australian Taxation Office was considering imposing tax on the income of charitable organisations, and in June 1990 it was realised that if legislation was passed the hospital could face a substantial tax bill. High interest rates meant that the hospital had accumulated some money which it needed to invest. A decision was made on the advice of Mr Roy Rothwell, the hospital's auditor, to invest in residential properties. Several were acquired including three in nearby Mary Street. One was a vacant block which was used as a car park for twelve staff cars. These acquisitions were to prove very useful during the rebuilding program nine years later when the premises were used as office accommodation, being only a minute's walk from the hospital.

Talbot Roy Rothwell was born in 1917. He worked for the firm of Walford, Rothwell and Treloar and was the League's auditor for approximately thirty years until his death in 1999. He had served in the Royal Australian Navy during the Second World War, and afterwards joined the Royal Australian Naval Volunteer Reserve, reaching the rank of lieutenant commander. He was always very interested in the hospital, and attended every annual general meeting.

Mr Roy Rothwell, hospital auditor, with Board member Mrs Sheila White, *Photo: Virginia Edwards.*

The early 1990s were not easy years for the hospital, and 1990 had a particularly bad start. Early in the year the Board decided to investigate malpractice insurance because 'there had been several recent incidents at the hospital'. In February there were long waiting periods. Changes to the rostering system, designed to improve this, only succeeded in exacerbating the situation. Some clients stopped attending. During the first six months of 1990 hospital receipts had decreased for the first time in eight years, with a drop of 1213 in the number of clients. Whereas receipts for the first six months of 1989 totalled $248,375, the amount for the same period in 1990 was $236,825, a drop of $11,550. There had been a significant rise in salary costs during this period, although other expenses had been well controlled.

Ten vets were employed, of whom one resigned in May 1990 because he had been intoxicated on duty. Relationships between the committee and the staff were strained. Initiative was not encouraged: the Board reprimanded the secretary for arranging, without permission, to have an exposed area of an office wall painted after a wall heater was moved. The demand by the Board that staff relinquish their on-site parking places to the Board members at meeting times met with antagonism. When the order was challenged the staff were told that parking on the premises was a privilege – the Board was not required to provide them with parking spaces.

In August 1990 a training program was introduced by a firm of management consultants. The aim was to bring closer cooperation between the various work groups, improve customer service and increase the staff awareness and appreciation of the role of the Lort Smith Animal Hospital in its service to the public and in animal welfare. The program cost $6000 and was held over an eight-week period. It used formal and informal group discussions and videotapes. Unfortunately the training was not as effective as had been hoped: a report by the consultants to the Board following the completion of the training stated that:

Because of the wide diversity of educational backgrounds and qualifications of your staff, the program utilised was beyond the scope of the original specifications and required a more concentrated approach by using a highly skilled professional trainer.

It was the first time such a training program had been run at the hospital. Possibly it was organised because of the recent introduction of the federal government's training guarantee legislation which required all employers with annual payrolls exceeding $200,000 to spend a minimum of 1%, later raised to 1.5%, of a company's payroll on staff training. For the hospital this amounted to $8000. Money not spent was either forfeited or donated to another institution for its use in an approved training program. Incidentally, in 1993, $7000 of unspent money was given to the Peter McCallum Institute (for cancer research) and the Guide Dogs Association.

In the early 1990s Dr Ruth King was appointed occupational health and safety officer. She attended a training course in mid 1991 and reported back to the committee. She made several suggestions regarding improving the safety of the working environment. These were accepted by the Board, which at this time was working on a redevelopment plan to extend the staff dining room and to build an additional storeroom. In April 1991 it was agreed that both projects proceed at a cost of $78,000 and the work was completed by October, under budget and ahead of time. The speed with which this had occurred was largely due to the diligence of Mr Alsop, who had had to deal with several bureaucratic delays and frustrations. Particularly irritating was the need to ask Melbourne City Council for a special dispensation because imperial measurements, which had been used in the original building, did not equate easily with the metric ones now being used in the renovation. As an example, special approval had to be obtained because the original stairway measured 920 millimetres in width instead of the standard 1000 millimetres.

In April 1991 a vet had his employment terminated because he 'appears to have a problem which may require psychiatric treatment'. He had been causing many difficulties with staff, including making physical threats, and he had written letters containing accusations about colleagues. In early 1992 this vet took the hospital to the Equal Opportunity Commission claiming that he had not been offered a permanent position because he had physical disabilities – a problem with his back. He claimed loss of wages of $1200 per week and $75,000 for personal suffering. The hospital denied that there had been a permanent position to offer him. The case was due to be heard when the hospital was informed that he had died so the matter would remain dormant. It was noted in the minutes, however, that the writing on the notification of death closely resembled that of the supposedly dead man, and there was a subsequent rumour that he had in fact falsely reported his own death.

In 1991 a serious conflict developed between the veterinary staff and the Board. The issues demonstrate the inevitable and ongoing tensions between the professional and administrative functions of the hospital. Vets view themselves as professionals, a status which carries with it the expectation of certain rights including the freedom to carry out their professional role without undue bureaucratic interference. Administrative functions of the hospital rely on the ability to quantify and control certain aspects of veterinary work. On 4 June 1991 the Board discussed the fact that staff, but particularly vets, were regularly late for work, and it was decided that time clocks be installed. One of the clocks was to be used for 'clocking on' and the second was installed in the surgical preparation room to record the length of time taken for cases where major surgery was required.

This provocative decision was perhaps influenced by the fact that the previous week two suitable clocks were offered at a receiver's auction at a local business for a total cost of $180 – it would have cost $2500 to buy these clocks new. No thought appears to have been given to the implications of making such a decision without warning or consultation – it was naively anticipated that 'it would be necessary to introduce the new time cards in tandum [sic] with the current "sign on" system for at least one period to ensure a smooth change over to the new system'.

The vets were upset that they had not been consulted. Dr Sequeira told the Board that the vets worked hard and it was his impression that those who had been late starters were no longer employed. He 'did not want to go back twelve months to restore the confidence in the relationship he had with his staff'. The Board countered this by saying that they treated the vets generously and that there had been no complaints over the recent pay rises. Dr Sequeira said that vets did not claim penalty rates for working on Sundays, but then it was pointed out that they were paid generously for working on public holidays. Dr Sequeira suggested the signing of a time sheet as a compromise, but the Board was adamant that the clocks be used, with one member suggesting that 'those who would not co-operate may like to look elsewhere for work', and another that the attitude of the vets was childish and 'maybe we should get rid of a few' and 'there was no shortage of vets at the present time'.

Several vets refused to use the clock, and when one vet requested leave to attend a training course on acupuncture in Sydney the decision was held over until a commitment had been received that she intended to comply with the instruction to clock-on.

The Board sought advice from various sources, but was informed by the Victorian Employers Federation that only staff employed under an award could be dismissed for failure to use the time clock as required by management. The Board decided that the hospital should draw up employment contracts which would require staff to work under any system the employer might require. The secretary was asked to investigate such a course of action.

A month after the system had been introduced only three vets were complying, and there was pressure on them by the other vets to cease doing so. Vets were signing their cards but not entering times. They were all issued with a draft employment agreement which made clocking-on a condition of employment.

The agreements were not finalised until December 1991, after considerable discussion including consultation with the vets. Some amendments were made at the request of the vets: they were to receive lawful direction from the secretary of the employer for all matters other than those of a veterinary nature; they were to be paid for the hours worked whereas previously they had worked certain hours for no payment; their sick-leave entitlements were to be brought into line with those of the rest of the staff; they were to receive two weeks' study leave each year on the proviso that it was scheduled so it did not interrupt the smooth running of the hospital; and a clause relating to the possession of intoxicating beverage on the premises was deleted.

In October 1992 it was reported that vets were still not using the time clocks, and Dr Sequeira was asked for an explanation. He explained that the vets were complying with item 4 of the Employer's Directions in their contracts which stated that they were required 'to complete time clock cards', which they were doing by signing the cards, as distinct from actually using the time clock. One member of the Board referred to this as 'childish', another said that as far as the committee was concerned if they chose not to use the clock perhaps they did not wish to be employed. Dr Sequeira agreed to convey the instruction of the committee to the vets, who replied that they would comply with their instruction but wished to express their disapproval and displeasure at having to do so – they found it demeaning and felt it questioned their honesty. This seems to have been the final episode in the clocking-on saga. The Board had won their battle, but the morale of the veterinary staff was badly dented.

In October 1991 Dr Sequeira had terminated the employment of one of the more experienced vets on the staff. No reason for this is recorded. The vet threatened action in the Supreme Court. No mention is made of the Board's view of this matter other than the comment that the decision taken by Dr Sequeira was 'reasonable'. The dispute was settled out of court, with the vet being paid three months' salary. No motion of the Board's support for Dr Sequeira is recorded after what must have been an intensely stressful event. The following month Dr Sequeira had concerns about the work of one of the veterinary nurses and sent him a letter outlining how he wished these concerns to be addressed. This led to further conflict. The matter was brought to the attention of the Board and the president interviewed the two staff members. The matter appears to have been a problem in communication between the two, but Dr Sequeira complained to the Board that he felt that he did not have its support, in which case he would have no option but to resign. He did not resign, but neither did the Board express their confidence in him. He made the same threat in May the following year when he was negotiating for a change of rostered hours. Had the issue of confidence and appropriate support been dealt with at any of these times Dr Sequeira's resignation from the position of senior vet one year later could perhaps have been avoided.

In May 1992 the Board was most disturbed by the number of complaints being made by dissatisfied clients, and decided to hold a special meeting. One such complaint was about a dog with a broken jaw being housed in a small cage in the cattery. Through a series of communication errors the owner had been informed that her dog had died, but it was found alive and well four days later.

The specific cases were discussed with Dr Sequeira who said that:

it was inevitable that mistakes would occur when such a large number of animals were treated each day – in fact he was surprised that it did not occur more often where such a large number of vets were concerned ... Many locums had been used lately because a number of permanent vets were on holidays or at seminars. The problem lay largely with the difficulty of conveying hospital procedures to locums and with the broken shifts required to fill the hours that the hospital was open for business.

He told the Board that two meetings of veterinary staff had been held in recent days and it was stressed that vets needed to follow established procedures and demonstrate a more caring attitude to owners.

The vets and members of the Board met on 26 May, when the president, Ian Dodd, did little more than repeat what Dr Sequeira had told the vets. The attitude of the Board was that such slip-ups would not be tolerated and staff who were not prepared to follow procedures would be dismissed. No consideration was given as to how the Board could assist in alleviating the high levels of stress the staff were experiencing.

It was also pointed out in the meeting that in the past year wages had been paid to over fifty vets, indicating a high use of locums which was expensive in salary costs as well as the administrative time required to teach and supervise them. The Board believed that twelve permanent staff should be adequate to fill the rostered times. It was agreed that a new roster of vets be drawn up.

Dr Sequeira, who had previously been working every Saturday, presented a new roster to the Board on 7 July. He told the Board that his previous working hours did not fit in with his private life and he felt he had earned the privilege of working only one Saturday each fortnight due to his eight or nine year employment history. He added that if this change were not agreed to he might be forced to resign. The Board accepted the roster at the next meeting but expressed concern at the amount of time that Dr Sequeira had off at weekends. Dr O'Riordan presented a letter on behalf of the vets supporting the revised roster and the changes to Dr Sequeira's working times because of his workload.

The roster was accepted with two conditions:

- Dr Sequeira was to be available to advise and solve problems at weekends (particularly at busy periods) and make unscheduled visits to the hospital
- A permanent roster was to be drawn up and it was to be a condition of employment of any new vet that they should take over an existing position on that roster

In February 1994 staff were working long hours, sometimes not finishing until 5 am. One presumes also that waiting times were long because it was recorded in February 1994 that a portable air-conditioner was to be purchased because clients were fainting at the weekend.

Things came to a head in 1993. Dr Sequeira was involved in an angry exchange with a client. The argument took place in a public area and was observed by staff and clients. The exchange demonstrated the extreme frustration of staff having to deal with the painful feelings of overwrought clients. When the committee reprimanded Dr Sequeira for the way he had handled the situation he resigned as senior vet, to be replaced by Dr Battaglene, but continued his employment at the hospital.

On 3 August 1993 Dr Battaglene told a Board meeting that he was pleased to have been appointed to the position of senior vet, but that he could hold the position only for a short period of time as he would be

Dr Alan Lawther, 1997, *Photo: Leader Community Newspapers.*

setting up his own practice in late September or early November. He also said that the hospital was currently held in very low esteem by the veterinary profession in general and that morale was very low among the hospital's veterinary staff. It was his intention to make the hospital a happier place for them to work. He expressed special concern about the quality of work of one vet, fairly recently appointed, and particularly criticised his theatre work. The Board, without any further investigation, decided that this vet should be dismissed.

Some of the vets reacted extremely angrily to the demotion of Dr Sequeira and the sacking of the junior vet, which was subsequently retracted. Eric Webb, who had recently taken over the presidency from Ian Dodd, described the situation as one of 'unprecedented unrest that could possibly lead to a walk out by several veterinary surgeons'.

Alan Lawther had sold his practice in 1990 and, because he missed his veterinary work, had returned to part-time work at the hospital shortly afterwards. When the conflict with the veterinary staff developed Eric Webb discussed the possibility of Alan's returning to the hospital as managing director, with a position on the Board. After some consideration Alan agreed to accept, although he suggested that he would be more comfortable with the title of veterinary director, a title he held until it was changed back to managing director in 1995 for reasons of protocol.

Alan's position was ratified at a Board meeting on 10 August 1993. It was his belief that some of the problems stemmed from there being a lay person in charge, and he felt it desirable to have a veterinary figure overseeing veterinary procedures. This view is shared by John Honey, who believes that there was a lack of clear boundaries between the administrative and the veterinary roles and that one of the problems which created conflict was that the position of José Sequeira was sometimes undermined by the secretary, Ron Joyce. Alan's promotion meant that the secretary would have a reduced workload, and since Ron Joyce was over seventy years of age it was considered an appropriate time for him to retire. The meeting agreed that 'a new secretary with knowledge of accountancy should be appointed and advertisements placed in national papers'. Unfortunately Ron Joyce's position was advertised before his retirement had been announced to the staff. At the next meeting, on 17 August, Eric Webb apologised for the embarrassment caused by this oversight. When the duties of the new secretary were brought up at the next Board meeting Mr Joyce said he wished to relinquish his position immediately, and left the premises.

At this time the management structure of the hospital underwent a fundamental change. John Honey became acting secretary until Susie Palmer took over in October 1993, but the duties formerly performed by Ron Joyce were split between the managing director and the secretary. John took a more direct role in the financial aspect of the hospital. Susie remained as secretary until June 1995. She was elected to the Board in early 1996. Soon after Alan took over as veterinary director in 1993 it was decided that Board meetings should be held once instead of twice a month because Alan was now dealing with many problems which had previously been referred to the Board. This arrangement started on a six-month trial basis and continued until recently when the number of meetings was again reduced. The Board now meets only once every two months.

On the advice of Alan Lawther, Dr Sequeira was reappointed senior vet on Dr Battaglene's departure and the staffing situation appears to have become more stable under Alan's leadership. In September 1994 Alan reported to the Board that there had been far fewer complaints than previously. However, the vets found the commercial aspect of quoting fees to clients was a problem and it was decided to buy printed pads on which vets could record different treatment options with their associated prices for clients to consider.

In January 1995 the Board engaged an independent adviser, Don McKenzie, from the firm of solicitors Sly & Weigall, to analyse and report on how to improve the functioning of the hospital. He made recommendations on the organisational structure, role definitions, enterprise agreements and the use of contracts for veterinary staff. The report was finished in March and as a result Alan's position was renamed managing director. There were also changes to the position of secretary (to be known as the manager-administration), the senior veterinary surgeon and the finance manager. Suggestions were made as to who should be delegated to interview for staff positions, and contracts for senior management positions were drafted. The resignation of Susie Palmer also prompted some changes to the organisational structure and John Honey was given the additional title of company secretary, which took over some of the duties of the role of manager-administration, and the new appointee, Janet Powell, was given the title of secretary. She was later replaced by Sasha Higgins.

On 2 June 1996 it was recorded in the minutes that 'there are no problems with the staff, it is a very good crew at the moment. Only one girl required a written warning because of habitual lateness'. And in September 1996 it was noted that 'there are few complaints these days; those that are received are dealt with quickly to the satisfaction of all concerned'.

In spite of this, in November 1996 the Board received a staff petition signed by forty-one staff members expressing dissatisfaction with working conditions. It pointed out that some staff who were not on award wages had not received a wage rise for over five years. It maintained that conditions for staff at the Lort Smith Hospital were more difficult than they were in private practice. Waiting times had increased, with clients having to wait four or five hours, putting staff under a lot of pressure. There was a further complaint that the Board members distanced themselves from the running of the hospital.

The Board reacted by immediately making changes to rectify the situation. They were not aware of the discontent among the staff and the procedures which had been agreed to for regular pay rises for vets had simply been overlooked, perhaps because the Board was too busy planning for the future to concern itself with the present. It was agreed that all staff not on an award rate should receive an annual cost-of-living adjustment, and that all vets who had completed the first three years of practice should receive a pay rise indexed to the cost of living, backdated to the last increase. It was also decided that a bonus system, to be paid on top of award rates, should be investigated.

To alleviate the waiting problem an extra surgery was created from the existing grooming room and an additional vet employed to help out in busy times. Additional clerical assistance was provided. Once again the decision was made that there should be greater communication with the staff, with a notice recording significant decisions made at Board meetings being displayed on the staff notice-board.

In April 1998 the vets again wrote to the Board regarding wage increases, and Alan Lawther reported that he had been discussing options regarding bonuses and productivity payments. The proposal which was finally accepted was peer appraisal, which proved effective but extremely time-consuming to administer. The Board was told in June 1999 that 'the bonus system is working well, with only one resignation since its introduction'.

The Board was becoming increasingly aware that the fabric of the hospital buildings was fast becoming a serious liability. The accommodation was cramped and in need of constant repair. Social expectations had also changed, and the hospital was competing with newer and better serviced veterinary clinics. Although the original building had been thoughtfully adapted with numerous modifications in response to the different pressures being placed upon it there came a time when a decision had to be made to rebuild.

The Board also took into account that the forthcoming legislation, the Companion Animals Act, required that animals not under treatment be kept in larger cages than the hospital was currently using. These could not be easily accommodated in the existing building. Larger cages were purchased, and a temporary extension was built to the cattery. The Act became law in early April 1996.

In March 1995 Dr Graeme Smith, Manager of the Lost Dogs' Home, offered the Lort Smith Hospital the opportunity to build on land which it held in Green Street. He believed that the public would benefit from amalgamating services on one site, and he was prepared to close down the hospital which was run by the Lost Dogs' Home in order to rationalise hospital services. Such a proposal would have saved a significant amount of money. The League decided not to accept this offer because it believed the proposal would threaten its autonomy.

Mr Eric Webb was delegated the task of approaching neighbours to see if they were prepared to sell. The time was opportune because, although prices in the area were rising, the sudden boom in land prices in North Melbourne was still a couple of years off. The hospital was interested in a property in Wreckyn Street which backed their current Villiers Street premises. The building was a factory/warehouse/office large enough to be subdivided to provide land for expansion while enabling the League to retain the Wreckyn Street frontage as a property which could be rented or sold at a later date. After many months of negotiation the purchase went through in May 1995 and planning for major rebuilding was able to commence.

The advantage of this purchase, as opposed to a property in Villiers Street, was that the site had sufficient depth to allow for a substantial modern building and a car park. It also enabled the hospital to retain the old hospital building. The upstairs caretaker's flat was renovated once the main building had been finished and the downstairs was turned into a centre for volunteers from which the pet therapy program and public relations events are now organised.

Historically the animal case histories had always been recorded by hand on individual cards which were about postcard size. In the 1980s a slightly larger card was used incorporating the KISS system which classified cards with coloured markers. But the incorrect filing of the cards sometimes made their retrieval difficult, and illegible handwriting occasionally meant that they were of little value. As the volume grew the cards had to be stored in various places all over the hospital which restricted space and made retrieval even more difficult. The result could be long waiting times while cards were searched for and inappropriate treatment when the cards were wrongly interpreted. Lost cards also meant a loss of income as cards were used to prove that a treatment had been provided when an owner denied that they had incurred a debt. Another possible threat from such a haphazard system was that the hospital could be sued for wrongful treatment.

With the growing belief that movement into a new building was inevitable, the Board appreciated that the adoption of a computerised record system would solve many problems. It was decided that this change should be implemented soon, before the move to the new hospital, to avoid the staff being confronted with too many changes at once. Considerable research was done into the different recording systems available and Vetaid was considered to be the clear favourite.

The Board decided to make the changeover time short and swift. For many of the staff the changeover was a leap into the dark as they were not familiar with the use of computers. It was also a complex task to adapt the available software to the particular needs of the hospital; previous records had been owner-based so were not readily available to deal with registering strays, and few practices which had already had computer programs installed had to deal with the Lort Smith's numbers of clients.

Alan Lawther describes the late November 1996 day when computerised recording was introduced:

Initially it was a disaster with threats of resignation starting at 8.40 am and several staff leaving early because of the chaos. Clients were lined up waiting for extended periods to be registered, consultations were extended as vets navigated the system, and the final insult was the client having to spend a further long wait to pay an account that could be outrageously incorrect either way. Often clients left without paying, their patience at an end.

That day will long be remembered by everyone rostered on.

Happily the end of the week saw improvements and by Christmas staff were feeling much more at ease with the system.

Once the decision was made to build, Dr John Hamilton from South Australia was asked to visit to advise on the new development. He had a great deal of experience both as a vet and as someone who had been involved through the Australian Veterinary Association in developing design guidelines for animal clinics. He had consulted on the building of around eighty new clinics. John completed plans for a land usage permit which, with the support of Lord Mayor Ivan Deveson and local councillor Lorna Hannan, were approved by Melbourne City Council.

Alan Lawther, who had an architectural background, with the assistance of John Honey, undertook an exhaustive process of selecting a Melbourne architect to work alongside Dr John Hamilton. They interviewed about eight architectural firms and visited their clients. They narrowed the field to four and invited them all to give a presentation to the Board. They finally selected the firm of Woodhead International because it had recently employed the architect John Reid who had been involved in the design of the University of Melbourne's College of Ophthalmology. The dean of the college was very enthusiastic about the design, and was also full of praise for the working relationship that had developed between him and the architect. The design was compatible with what Alan had envisaged for the Lort Smith, and so the decision was made and ratified by the Board.

Woodhead International was appointed on 2 December 1997. Alan Lawther, John Honey and, initially, Dr John Hamilton worked closely with the architects to develop their brief and John Honey was amazed at how time-consuming this process was. It was a one-off building designed from scratch, and the process took up forty full-day sessions. Alan Lawther's architectural knowledge came in very useful. The choice of architect was a good one. John Reid's work was excellent, though it was unfortunate that he was taken ill about two-thirds of the way through the project; his role was taken over by his brother, Graham Reid.

The administrative staff moved to the Mary Street property in April 1998 to allow building to start, but the animal treatment areas remained in the old building. The facility was being rebuilt because it was too small; to continue practising in a space of less than one third of that, even on a temporary basis, presented many problems. The boardroom became the cattery while the garage and staff-room were used to house the dogs. New stainless steel cages had been bought for the new hospital and Alan Lawther commented that:

even with the chaos of demolition all around the sight of those sparkling cages gave everyone a glimpse of the facility to come, easing the pain of the surrounds.

The two outdoor areas of the puppy yard and the casting lawn were a godsend. Two temporary sheds were placed on each of these. Those on the lawn became the two surgical theatres while those in the puppy yard housed cats and isolation cases respectively ... X-rays had to be done in a converted consultation room which was some distance from the surgeries and theatres and which was accessible only by an uncovered route.

Whilst the renovations were being carried out only one operating theatre was available, putting the hospital under considerable pressure. Dr Cimati volunteered to help out by doing some surgery at his private practice in Brunswick for the same price as the hospital charged.

The only major delay to the rebuilding was caused by the discovery of contaminated soil; this had to be removed with special precautions in place and this significantly contributed to the cost.

Lobbying for animal welfare organisations to receive tax deductibility continued during the 1990s and this is dealt with in more detail in chapter twelve. The Board experienced what turned out to be a major disappointment in this regard. The tax office informed the League in May 1996 that it had achieved its aim of having donations made tax deductible. This followed many years of lobbying and came at a time when donations were urgently needed to boost the appeal fund. The Board celebrated with champagne – though only one bottle between them all! Three weeks later the decision was reversed – only the few people who had made donations during this three-week period were able to claim a tax deduction. The reason for the decision was that the hospital deals with 'non-human beneficiaries'. The battle continues.

Mrs Susie Palmer, Mr Eric Webb, Mr John Honey, Dr Alan Lawther and Mrs Virginia Edwards relax after the 1995 AGM, *Photo: Lort Smith Animal Hospital.*

The hospital did have one win however, being granted exemption from payroll tax, a decision which was made retrospective for three years through the endeavours of John Honey. When he was thanked by the Board he was also commended on his latest budget, which the minutes said 'was very closely managed'.

One of the dilemmas faced by John Honey and the Board was how to finance the building. By 3 July 1997 the $1 million loan taken out on the Wreckyn Street property was nearly paid off through bequests and donations. The decision was taken to sell all properties except those in Mary Street and Wreckyn Street. The Board finally took out a loan for $2 million repayable over fifteen years to finance the building. This will be repaid largely from the legacies which the hospital continues to receive. Much of the credit for this source of income has to be given to Sadie Howe who, as already mentioned, was relentless in her search for generous bequests.

Among the substantial donations which the hospital received during this period was a grant of $200,000 by the Sidney Myer Centenary Celebration 1899-1999 towards the rebuilding of the hospital. This was to be distributed over a period of four years between 1999 and 2003. The late Yasuko Hiraoka Myer, wife of Kenneth Myer, had donated regularly to the hospital during her lifetime. Both died tragically in an aircraft accident in July 1992. The hospital received a generous bequest under the terms of her will.

Income from several trusts from the estates of benefactors, including Lady Lyle and Mrs Lort Smith, continue to generate money for the hospital on an annual basis.

Once the Board had decided, after much consideration, to employ a professional fundraiser, a fundraising committee convened by Virginia Edwards considered different fundraising consultants. Downes Venn and Associates was appointed. The company presented a feasibility study in September 1997 and suggested that two or three high-profile people were needed to give their financial support during the appeal. Unfortunately attempts to interest several people in such a role failed.

Stage one was the newsletter for Christmas 1997. It was designed and laid out by Downes Venn which arranged its distribution. The cost of the mail-out was $9615 and it was hoped that $15,000 would be raised. By the time of the Board meeting in February $16,520 had been raised, giving the hospital a total profit of $6905.

Downes Venn made a presentation to the Board in April saying that it was arranging for invitations to be sent to prospective donors to attend various functions at which they would be told about the plans for the new hospital. However, they needed more names of prospective donors, and they emphasised the need for the Board to encourage the promotion by giving generously themselves and asking their friends to do so. As the first stage of the promotion was behind schedule the firm offered to extend its services by an extra three months at no charge. Promotional material was sent out, but the only response received was from Ms Jenny Wickham, executive assistant of Tattersall's. She was impressed by her visit to the hospital and Tattersall's pledged $10,000 toward the pet therapy program and also promised to assist through advertising the building appeal.

The outcome of the appeal was most unsatisfactory, despite assurances from the fundraiser that things would improve. In October

1998 the Board was told that there was $142,000 in confirmed pledges, $155,000 in intended pledges and $125,000 in promised gifts in kind. In December 1998 the accounts showed that expenditure paid to Downes Venn was $74,000 plus $27,492 for mail-outs and $2356 for brochures and printing-a total of $103,848. This expenditure had raised only $53,837, a shortfall of $50,011. They had virtually no success in selling naming rights to the hospital. Their efforts were to cost the hospital more money than they recovered, and Virginia Edwards spoke of this in her forthright manner when she was interviewed for the documentary film 'The Loved Ones' (discussed in the next chapter). Virginia pulled no punches when she expressed her views, and was described by its maker, Kate Hampel, as 'really gutsy' in an interview with Nicole Brady published in *The Age's Green Guide* after the film had been shown publicly.

Councillor Lorna Hannan launched the new hospital on 10 March 1999 by unveiling a bronze plaque. She had been most helpful to the Board and had assisted in smoothing the way with the Melbourne City Council. A marquee was erected and afternoon tea was served.

Mr Greg Champion with Julius Palmer at the launch of the new hospital, 10 March 1999, *Photo: Lort Smith Animal Hospital.*

The occasion was hosted by Magda Szubanski, well known comedian and star of the 1995 movie 'Babe'. Greg Champion performed a song he had specially written for the occasion. Called 'For the Animals', it told the stories of animals who had been written about in the hospital newsletter.

Ms Magda Szubanski at the launch of the new hospital, 10 March 1999, *Photo: Lort Smith Animal Hospital.*

8 Into the future

The newly constructed hospital, 1999, *Photo: Keith Bedford.*

The move to the new premises brought additional challenges. How the clientele would feel about the new hospital was a major preoccupation of the Board before the opening– would they be put off by a perception that it was too 'grand'? Would they perceive that too much had been spent on the administrative facilities at the expense of the diagnostic and treatment programs? Another challenge was how to deal with the uncertainty of operating costs in the more technically sophisticated building.

It had been hoped that the hospital would start the year 2000 in its new building, but the delay associated with contaminated soil meant that this was not to be and the ultimate date of completion was 16 June 2000. The move to the new building took place from Monday to Thursday of the following week, although it took a couple more weeks for the building to be fully operational. The new hospital was open for business on 23 June. The move demonstrated how the staff team could work well together with a common goal and common purpose. There was little disruption to the hospital schedule other than the cessation of all but emergency operations, but vets were required to work additional hours, and two extra vets were employed to assist. There were inevitable problems with delivery of equipment and furnishings, and at times the staff had to 'make do'. The power failed twice in one day.

An additional twenty-four new computers were installed, bringing the total to about fifty. On one occasion the computer system crashed due to overload. The move took place shortly before the introduction of the goods and services tax so there was the additional task of making the computer system GST compliant.

The first Board meeting was held without a board table– the old one was too small to seat all Board members, and a new one was being purchased. But more symbolically, for the first time there were no permanent seating arrangements as had been the case in past years, when each new member was allocated a seat and remained in that place until he or she retired.

The official opening took place on 24 November 2000. Unfortunately the Governor of Victoria, Sir James Gobbo, who intended to officiate, had taken ill while overseas and was unable to attend. The Honourable Jeffrey Kennett, who had been the Liberal Premier under the previous state government agreed, at very short notice, to open the hospital. Mr Kennett, who is interested in the issue of depressive illnesses in the community and is very involved in the charity 'Beyond Blue', emphasised the important role that animals play in the lives of the old, the ill and the lonely and how they provide some people with their only motivation for living. He recounted one owner telling him that it was only the concern for her pet that had prevented her taking her life. He praised the volunteers in particular, saying that they were the main driving force in most charities, and believed their advocacy of their cause is one of the most important activities in any community. In many cases the effect of advocacy in influencing people's value systems and in disseminating information was of greater value than the actual service being given. He concluded by saying how much he felt the League had achieved, and how impressed he was that the Board had taken on the responsibility of building the new hospital without any government funding.

Mr David White and Mr Jeff Kennett at the hospital opening, *Photo: Keith Bedford.*

Mr David White, Mr Jim Wilson and Mr Jeff Kennett admire the old ambulance, *Photo: Keith Bedford.*

There were several changes to the Board in 2000. Sadie Howe resigned her position in April due to poor health, but retained her honorary title of President Emeritus. David White took over as chairman when Eric Webb resigned in March 2000 after seven years in that position. Maggie Allmand and Rick Macdonald were elected vice-presidents and Susie Palmer was elected treasurer. Eric completed one more year on the Board in 2001.

Ian Dodd died on 21 February 2000. He had replaced Sadie Howe as president in 1989 but following his diagnosis of Parkinson's disease he resigned from the position in 1993, although he remained on the Board until his death. David Alsop gave a moving eulogy at his funeral. His obituary in the hospital newsletter recorded that:

Ian's sense of humour, outstanding feeling and understanding of Hospital issues and excellent judgement remained with him until the end.

Samantha Baillieu joined the Board in June 2000.

Alan Lawther had retired from his position as managing director in February 2000 due to ill health but remained a very active Board member. He had originally planned to remain in the position until the new hospital was completed and he felt it would be advisable to have time to work beside his successor. Unfortunately Alan's continuing ill health meant that he had to leave several weeks before the new

Mr Ian Dodd, President of the Board of Management 1989-1993, *Photo: Lort Smith Animal Hospital.*

building was finished. He was replaced by Jim Wilson. When Alan was well enough he enjoyed spending time at the hospital doing maintenance tasks including making cages for the cattery. After retirement Alan's health made a dramatic improvement, and he returned briefly to his previous administrative position on a part-time basis between October 2001 and February 2002 following Jim Wilson's resignation.

Kate Hampel, a young Melbourne film-maker who had visited the Lort Smith Animal Hospital as a child, was interested in researching the history and operation of the hospital to create a documentary. The Board agreed to her project in June 1998. The film was to cover the history of the hospital, its long-term clients and the part the hospital plays in the wider community. It was also to focus on the hospital's services and lead up to the launch of the building appeal. Kate was able to get funding for her fifty-five minute film, to be shown on the ABC.

A private showing of 'The Loved Ones' at the State Film Centre in November 1999 raised a good deal of consternation in both staff and Board members. The staff felt aggrieved by some of the comments and Dr Fiona Anderson approached the Board about some of the issues raised and the reaction of the staff to the film. Virginia Edwards, the one Board member who had been particularly outspoken in the film, was asked by the president to write to each of the veterinary staff members individually to say that her comments in the documentary were not the sentiments of the Board.

The Board felt that the hospital had not been portrayed in a positive way, and tried to negotiate to have changes made. Susie Palmer convened a meeting of herself, solicitor Nathan Kuperholz, acting in a pro-bono capacity, and the film's producer and director. The Board were hoping that there would be room for negotiation as to what was to be included but in fact this was non-negotiable. A compromise agreement was made that a statement could be inserted before the commencement of the film which would take three or four seconds to read and would cost the hospital $380. This read: 'The new Lort Smith Animal Hospital will open in May 2000'.

The public reaction to the film when it was shown on 26 April 2000 resulted in a significant increase in donations and raised the profile of the hospital in a way which had not been foreseen. On 2 May 2000 it was reported in the minutes that donations were currently $8696. The total raised through the screening was approximately $30,000, but other gifts were received from the public such as several parcels of clothes beautifully made by a woman in New South Wales.

Staffing issues held centre stage at the beginning of the year. One of the first matters addressed during the first Board meeting of the twenty-first century was the list of concerns raised by staff as a result of 'The Loved Ones', and in particular the question of how to foster a closer relationship between the staff and the Board. One suggestion was that new vets be introduced to the Board – a decision which had been made on several previous occasions during the history of the hospital when morale had been low.

The hospital's staffing structure was also discussed after it became known that Dr José Sequeira had expressed his intention of resigning. The Board acknowledged that his experience was invaluable to the hospital, and it was suggested that he should be offered a new position of consultant vet, and that two additional positions of head vet should be created. This meeting also decided to ask the vets to select a liaison person to attend Board meetings on a regular basis by invitation. The vets subsequently decided that communication with the Board should go through Dr Sequeira, and in the event of a dispute with him the vets would appoint another of their number to represent them.

A special Board meeting was held on 18 January 2000 which confirmed the suggestion made at the previous meeting that the veterinary stream should have three senior positions – a director of veterinary services, responsible for clinical services and training of veterinary staff, under whom would be two senior vets who would work alternate weekends. It was resolved that Dr Sequeira should be offered the position of director of veterinary services following an assurance from Dr Lawther that he had proved himself to be excellent at training staff.

Twelve applications had been received for the position of managing director, and the short listing and interviewing had already taken place. The position was to encompass marketing, public relations, human resources and education, and the appointee would be responsible for the director of veterinary services and the finance manager and would oversee the administrative functions of the hospital. The salary package was to be negotiated, and would include an annual bonus according to income performance results. It was agreed that one of the short listed candidates, Jim Wilson, should be offered the position.

Both Jim Wilson and José Sequeira accepted their appointments, with Dr Sequeira making the proviso that he would reassess his position when the new CEO had settled in. Appointments to the newly created positions of senior vet were made in May 2000. Dr Patrick Cheah and Dr Fiona Anderson were each to work a four-day week with alternate weekends.

Jim Wilson started as Managing Director in March. There was little time for Alan Lawther to show him the ropes as Alan's health was deteriorating sharply, and he resigned within a short time of Jim's arrival.

Shortly after the move to the new hospital, on 21 July 2000, José Sequeira gave in his notice after seventeen-and-a-half years of service, having been in charge of the hospital's veterinary work for the previous ten years. He excelled as a surgeon, was always ready to give the benefit of his knowledge and skills to less experienced vets who worked under him, and raised the profile of the hospital. After his resignation he returned to work in his home country, East Timor, which had recently obtained its independence.

The Board received his resignation with regret. The members took the opportunity to review the different options for the hospital's organisational structure, and it was decided that the position of director of veterinary services should be split into two. Directors were to be appointed over two streams: veterinary medicine and veterinary surgery. The decision was challenged at the next Board meeting as being too costly. It had been common for decisions made at previous meetings to be questioned, debated and overturned. On this occasion David White as chairman took a firm stand. He acknowledged the concern but pointed out that the matter had been fully discussed at the previous Board meeting. He maintained that it was necessary to adhere to decisions that had been made to ensure effective operation of the hospital.

Staff and Board members celebrate in the new staffroom, December 2000, *Photo: Lort Smith Animal Hospital.*

The new staffing structure came into effect in November 2000 with the following appointments:

Head of Veterinary Medicine	Dr Harold Pook
Deputy Head of Veterinary Medicine	Dr Jacqui Moore
Head of Surgery	Dr Patrick Cheah
Deputy Head of Surgery	Dr Gary Oakes

In August 2000 Dr Lawther informed the Board that the waiting time for clients had increased since the move to the new premises. It had been hoped that one vet would be able to service two surgeries but this was not happening. The reception staff were finding it difficult to cope with the frustrations of the waiting public.

He also reported an undercurrent of unrest amongst the staff and predicted the likelihood of further resignations by key staff unless this was addressed. He suggested the appointment of male and female liaison officers from the Board to listen to staffing problems. However, Jim Wilson opposed this suggestion, saying that he had an open-door policy and that any member of staff could approach him at any time. Jim mentioned that there had been an offer from two human resource consultants to donate their time to help form a staff consultative committee. This committee would hold monthly meetings and address issues such as future directions, occupational health and safety, and other policy, procedural and operational issues. Whilst this committee did operate for a while the staff felt it was ineffective – issues would be brought up but not resolved.

A further suggestion was made and accepted that a liaison officer be elected and nominated by the staff to mediate on any problems or matters of concern. This was essentially an identical decision to that which had been made in January of the same year but which had not been implemented because the vets had agreed to liaise with the Board through José Sequeira. Things had changed with the appointment of Jim Wilson and the decision appears to have been overlooked.

Another important need was for the hospital to update its information technology, particularly focusing on the development of email and internet connections and the upgrading of its technological resources. Michael Curry, who had been a veterinary nurse since 1994, was appointed to this task. He had developed a keen interest in information technology and taught himself the basics of user support so that in 1999 he was able to obtain a position with the software developer Vetaid, where he widened his knowledge and skills. Michael was promoted to the position of information technology manager in May 2000 and the hospital paid for him to obtain a technology qualification in a course run by Microsoft. Michael has gradually extended the use of information technology to help streamline processes such as the downloading of diagnostic results from the external pathology laboratory directly onto a client's file.

Jim Wilson resigned as managing director in October 2001. Alan Lawther returned to the position temporarily while a replacement was sought, and Peter Brown started on 18 February 2002, albeit under a different title – the position was redesignated general manager. Alan Lawther was able to enjoy his retirement once again.

The Lort Smith Hospital appeals to veterinarians for several different reasons – including sometimes the scarcity of jobs elsewhere, and the considerable expense of buying into private practice. Many join because they are altruistic about animal welfare, others because they like to be part of a large group of staff and there are few other places where this can happen. Vets at the hospital have a wide and busy case load so they are able to gain experience in a range of treatments and procedures. Nurses and other support staff join for the same reasons.

Staff have also left for many different reasons, often personal. But staff exit surveys conducted in 2001 by human relations professionals indicate that pay and working conditions are very important. One of the senior vets believes that:

Historically there was the perception of an attitude from management that the staff were dispensable and that they could be easily replaced. It was not expected that the staff would remain in the LSAH for more than a few years. This has led to the strong feeling that the staff are poorly valued by management and has led to issues of poor staff morale.

One of the strengths of the Lort Smith Animal Hospital is the quality of its surgeons, many of whom have developed high levels of skill.

The hospital, according to Dr Harold Pook, probably does more orthopaedic surgery than any other general private practice in Melbourne, so there is always the opportunity for staff to extend their knowledge and experience. Another strength is that there are some vets at the hospital with specialised interests and skills, for instance orthopaedic surgery, cancer management, dental procedures and treatment of birds, who are available for consultation.

Dr Harold Pook began work at the Lort Smith in 1997 as a specialist consultant. He later took on the part-time position of head of veterinary medicine, but resigned after ten months due to the difficulty of combining this role with outside business commitments. He also held some philosophical positions which differed from those of the Board. He did not believe these differences could be resolved in the short term and this would have made an ongoing working relationship extremely difficult.

During his tenure he brought about some significant changes which included the introduction of the intensive care unit, the implementation of an appointment system, changes to the staffing levels and organisation of shifts to reduce staff stress and the amount of overtime. These changes had a beneficial effect on client waiting times and effectiveness of treatment.

Dr Pook now holds the position of consulting vet, and attends regularly to advise staff on medical and dental problems and treatment. His expertise gives the hospital access to ultrasound, endoscopy, chemotherapy, and advanced case assessment. Management of the more complicated medical and dental cases seen at the hospital would otherwise have to be referred elsewhere or animals perhaps euthanased because the owners would not be able to afford treatment at other veterinary centres.

The new facilities have improved the overall level of comfort for patients and owners. The implementation of the appointment system has reduced average waiting times.

In 2001 the intensive care unit, staffed seven days a week, was opened. This means that very sick animals requiring intensive management get constant and specialised care for at least part of the day, which is not usually the case in general practice, although animals which require twenty-four hour intensive care have to be referred elsewhere. The unit has brought about a dramatic improvement in the level of care provided to sick animals and those recovering from surgery. Fluid therapy, blood products and a ventilator to assist animals with respiratory problems have been introduced into the new facility. Another improvement has been in the communication between staff and owners.

Although the Board has always tried to ensure that there is adequate equipment it is costly and has to be shared among many staff. According to Dr Harold Pook:

There is always a need for more basic and advanced equipment – for instance, newer or more ophthalmoscopes, otoscopes, dental equipment, surgical equipment. The Lort Smith Animal Hospital would also benefit from on site advanced equipment like endoscopes, ultrasound machines, blood analysers etc. However, there are big issues with such equipment such as the necessity of training staff to use it efficiently and the time required to use and maintain the equipment. Already there is a large time pressure on staff. Having visiting consultants come to the Lort Smith Animal Hospital provides access to supplementary skills and equipment which enhance the services which are provided 'in house'.

(An endoscope is an instrument which allows an internal inspection of the digestive tract and stomach to be carried out by inserting a tube through an animal's mouth. An otoscope is used to examine ears and an ophthalmoscope is for examining eyes.)

Dr Pook believes that training for nursing staff needs to be reviewed, as many vet nurses have been volunteers who have relied on gaining their knowledge and skills through on-the-job training. While such training is very valuable, reliance on this form alone has reduced the benefits which come from the 'cross-pollination' of nursing and kennel staff, and has tended to limit professional growth within the hospital. Efforts to redress this are being made, and several of the recently hired nurses are enrolled in formal nursing diploma courses. Dr Pook also acknowledges that the work at the Lort Smith is relatively more stressful than in other clinics, with longer hours, more demanding and difficult clients and until recently, poor facilities.

An innovation in 2001 was the introduction of a free psychological/counselling service provided at the hospital by the Cairnmillar Institute for both staff and clients of the hospital. The service is provided one day a week through the institute's intern program.

Relationships with the veterinary profession

The veterinary profession has held an ambivalent attitude to the Animal Welfare League from its inception. Whilst recognising that there was a genuine need to give the less well-off access to free or discounted veterinary treatment, there was also the fear that any institution which set itself up for this purpose would threaten the livelihood of private practitioners, and that the system would be open to abuse by those who could afford to pay. Dr Alan Lawther has an interesting observation about the way in which, like doctors, vets used to charge their patients in guineas. He believed this was possibly done to maintain 'mystique' and bolster professionalism.

The League faced opposition from members of the Victorian branch of the Australian Veterinary Association (AVA) even before the clinic opened. Mr Hector Kendall operated a private practice in Brunswick Street, Fitzroy on the site where his father had opened the first animal hospital in 1888. He told an AVA meeting in 1929 when the proposed clinic was being discussed that he, being the nearest vet, would be hardest hit. He mentioned that when the Veterinary School clinic had closed he had experienced a great increase in small animals at his practice. He suggested a ticket system for needy people who could receive free treatment from any veterinarian in the scheme, and said that he had himself treated the animals of poor people without charge. He suggested as an alternative a roster of vets at the clinic so that no pecuniary or publicity advantage should be gained by one vet at the expense of another.

Dr Bordeaux told the meeting that he felt that a roster system would be unworkable because of the degree of co-operation required for it to work. He also said that he had attended several meetings in connection with the proposed clinic and had already been asked to act as the League's veterinary officer. He was convinced that the League would open its own clinic whether or not it had the co-operation of the university. The meeting decided to support the proposal to open a free clinic at the Veterinary School, but also asked that the idea of a roster system for veterinary services be considered.

After the League's clinic opened, complaints from members of the Victorian Veterinary Association continued. It was alleged at an association meeting in December 1930 that 'the [AWL] Hospital was admitting the animals of people who were in a position to pay for a veterinarian, and further that certain charges were being made which were sometimes as much as the fee a veterinarian would charge a client, and that therefore the League was not a charitable institution for poor people'.

In March 1931 it was decided that the university would employ a person who would interview people seeking treatment and turn away those able to pay fees. A person claiming treatment would be asked to sign a declaration stating that their income did not exceed the basic wage, and the maximum charge for the use of the ambulance would be five shillings. In September 1933, after further concern by the veterinary fraternity, a registrar was appointed by the university council to reinforce the conditions.

With the opening of the new hospital the vetting of clients was obviously not so stringent, and in February 1936 Lady Fairbairn suggested that, rather than record the names and addresses of the owners of dogs receiving treatment, the dogs' cards should be numbered. This 'would not give the Vets cause for complaints regarding the treatment of animals of people living in such suburbs as Toorak'.

Eight years after the Animal Welfare League had opened its first clinic its activities were still viewed with suspicion. Mrs Norman Brookes made this appeal at the League's annual general meeting in 1938:

We must try to gain the support of the veterinary surgeons. I don't know why they should be against this concern: medical men generally take an interest in the work done by the hospitals for the sick poor and I see no reason why the Animal Welfare League and the veterinary surgeons should not work together.

The active attempt in 1943 by some senior AVA members to impede the running of the hospital and to bring about its amalgamation with the VSPA was discussed in detail in chapter four.

In November 1953 Ann Flashman, a private veterinary practitioner who was an active member of the AVA, had sent a cat to the hospital for treatment and it was put down without any prior discussion with her. She complained to the Board and said that she would not send any further animals to the hospital. On two occasions in the 1960s she was offered a place on the Board but she declined on both occasions.

Ann Flashman became Lady Rylah when she married Sir Arthur Rylah (1909-74) a prominent politician who was Attorney General 1955-67 and later Deputy Premier and Chief Secretary. She was well known for her column on animal welfare in the *Herald*. She died in 1969.

In November 1954 the Victorian Practitioners Association offered to staff the hospital with a panel of the association members who would supply a full-time honorary service. Correspondence on the matter was accepted but no discussion recorded.

In 1956 legislation was passed amending the Veterinary Surgeons Act. It set up the Veterinary Board, giving it wide powers to control advertising, and power to suspend or cancel the registration of any vet. Its regulations prevented the hospital advertising under the wording 'Veterinary Hospitals', but it was allowed to appear in the Pink Pages of the telephone directory under the heading 'Animal Hospitals'. However, it was not until the 1980s that the Veterinary Board really began trying to wield its extra power in an attempt to bring the League and other institutions such as the RSPCA into line.

In March 1960 the hospital experienced a serious crisis with the staffing of its night clinic, and the Board's immediate decision was to close it. This decision was rescinded at the next meeting. The night clinic was very dear to the Board members. They had fought hard to establish it and were prepared to continue the fight to keep it going just as they were when faced with a similar predicament in 1957.

A week after the decision had been made to close the night clinic an emergency meeting was held at the hospital to which Mr Crowther and Mr Booth were invited. The Board told them that it was keen to overturn its previous decision even if this meant some cuts to the day services including the ambulance service and the pharmacy. It was even prepared to consider the boarding of dogs, an arrangement which it had strongly resisted in the past. It asked the finance committee to advise and to report back within two weeks.

In the meantime it was mooted that the Victorian branch of the AVA should take over the hospital's emergency services. The finance advisory committee was strongly supportive of such a move and advised the Board to *'stress that it did not wish to compete with private surgeons or the Veterinary Association, its prime consideration being the availability of professional services for animals on the widest possible basis'*.

The Board had always been fiercely protective of its autonomy, and would have been genuinely threatened by this proposal. However, the situation was so critical that it had to be seriously considered, and the Board agreed to have discussions with the Victorian Practitioners Association which was simultaneously offering to come to such an arrangement with the League through its spokesman, Mr Blogg. On 7 June 1960 Mr Blogg told the League that 'a number of private Veterinary Surgeons were starting emergency clinics at week-ends and public holidays on a zonal basis and had offered to help the Lort Smith Hospital if terms and conditions could be agreed'.

In September 1960 the proposals of the Veterinary Practitioners Association were put to the Board. It offered to staff all weekend and holiday clinics, maintaining the current hours of operation. It would provide locums if any of its regular vets were sick or on holiday, and guarantee these conditions 'on a permanent basis for some years to come'. It agreed to arrange all the rosters and treat all cases brought to the hospital, whether emergencies or not. It would observe and obey all the rules and regulations of the hospital. This seems to have been a generous offer, very advantageous to the League.

Dame Mabel Brookes, Mrs Nelken, Mrs Trathan and Mr Moreton met with VPA representatives in September to discuss plans for cooperation in more detail. At the time the situation looked serious because the vet who had run the weekend and night clinic since May

1960, Mr Stack, had twice threatened to walk out, and his assistant had complained about his conduct. An in-principle agreement was reached about the way in which arrangements should take place, the details of which were put to a Board meeting on 23 September, together with a recommendation from Mr Crowther that the League should ratify the agreement. Indeed the Board did agree to accept the recommendations although the financial aspects of it were still to be negotiated with the VPA secretary, Mr Gannon.

The deal stalled because Mr Stack did not immediately go ahead with his threat to leave. The VPA was asked to wait until his position was clarified. When Mr Stack left approximately two weeks later the Board appointed a new vet from Sydney, Mr Neasey, and Mr Pulvirenti conducted the night and weekend clinic on a greatly reduced basis until Mr Neasey could take up his appointment.

On 26 October 1960 Dame Mabel and Mr Moreton attended a meeting with representatives from the Veterinary Practitioners Association. The proposal was made that the Metropolitan Practitioners Association (the group covering the inner city area in which the hospital was situated) should completely staff the hospital on an honorary basis, and that the hospital should almonise (decide on the ability of a client to pay fees) all cases and accept only those where no charge or reduced charges would apply. This would mean that only cases where the patient's owner could not afford normal veterinary fees would be eligible for treatment. This proposal was rejected by the Board following discussion with Mr Crowther.

It is hardly surprising, given its history, that the League was prepared to muddle along and retain its autonomy rather than enter into an arrangement with the VPA, however advantageous. Neither is it surprising that the staffing situation continued to lurch from one crisis to another. Mr Neasey stayed for less than two months and apparently left under a cloud. He was asked to leave the hospital on the day he handed in his notice, and although the salary owed to him for his period of notice was to be paid he was to have one-and-a-half days' pay deducted from his salary. Mr Tudhope had already given his notice and was to leave on 3 February 1961.

The matter of cooperation between the VPA and the League was not mentioned again.

The vet Don Tynan, who worked at the Lort Smith Animal Hospital between 1964 and 1968 and again briefly in the early 1970s, expressed these thoughts on the relationship between the hospital and the wider veterinary profession:

The question of Animal Hospital practice and private practice was never far away. At the early stages of my involvement I felt disapproval amongst practitioners of the 'competition', even 'unfair competition' that the Lort Smith Animal Hospital was offering. In what way did this come about? The LSAH had a public face, a good sense of public relations and some freedom to rise above the conservative and stifling restrictions on advertising by private practitioners. It had a significant building – when veterinary hospitals elsewhere were rare. It had conspicuous ambulances on the roads of every suburb, seven days a week, and word of mouth recommendation amongst the public.

This fear of competition influenced the AVA to maintain a strict policy that spaying and vaccinations should not be undertaken at the Lort Smith Animal Hospital. However, in 1962 the hospital began to challenge the Association's ruling on spaying, and on 21 August 1962 the Board told the vets that 'it is the wish of the Council that all kittens old enough to be castrated be operated on before they leave the Hospital for homes'. On 4 December 1962 the secretary was told to write to the AVA informing it of the council's decision to spay and immunise approximately twenty dogs per week. These decisions seem to have been taken without consultation with the hospital's vets.

On 2 July 1963 the AVA apologised for the six-month delay in replying to the League's December letter and advised that in its opinion the Lort Smith Hospital should not undertake to spay animals as 'it would surely be outside the hospital's true function'. It was agreed that the secretary should write to ask the association if there would be any private vet prepared to spay pensioners' animals at a reduced charge. No reply to this letter was recorded.

On 20 July 1965 Dr Alan Lawther asked the Board to clarify its policy on spaying and immunisation. He said that the Victorian

Practitioners Association was concerned at the report that spaying and immunisation was done at the hospital, and if this was the case the hospital would find it difficult to replace veterinary surgeons. Alan also said he felt strongly that it was unethical for a vet to spay patients from another district. The Board replied that 'it was not the Hospital's policy to spay and immunise but that nothing could be done to prevent staff members, in their desire to help the public, from suggesting any particular Veterinary Surgeon'.

Don Tynan was convinced that the ban on live vaccination caused animals and their owners much unnecessary suffering and he decided to challenge it. He bought a supply of vaccine to protect against distemper and feline enteritis from a local supplier and used this on all animals brought to the hospital which appeared to be clinically normal. He described the results as 'amazing', with a huge reduction in the number of animals which had to be returned because they were sick or dying, and avoiding subsequent costly treatment with drugs such as antibiotics.

Having come from the country, and not having practised in Melbourne previously, he had not considered the reaction of the AVA. He was summoned to a meeting at the Victorian Research Institute with the president of the Victorian Division, Evans Jones (T. E. Jones), and someone else representing the Practitioners Branch, where he was told that he 'was defying the whole of the veterinary profession' with his stance. In his own words: 'however, upsetting as it was to incur such wrath, I said that I could not ethically do otherwise, and left. As far as I know, no other action followed, and after 1968 I left Melbourne...'

On 14 February 1967 the League wrote to the AVA informing it of the League's intention to spay and immunise dogs and cats and the reply was a request for a meeting. An informal meeting took place on 17 March with Dame Mabel Brookes, Mrs Howe, Dr J. W. Watson BVSc (president of the AVA), Miss Ann Flashman and Mr T. E. Jones. The League's minutes record that 'a good atmosphere prevailed and several points of interest were discussed'. The association acknowledged the financial problem facing the League and was anxious for the hospital to continue in view of the assistance given to people of small means. They were in favour of spaying and immunisation to a limited degree but charges should be comparable with those of private practitioners except in the case of pensioners. The meeting concluded with the agreement that a letter was to be written by Dame Brookes and Sadie Howe on behalf of the AWL notifying the AVA of the views of the Board – in the meantime no spaying or immunising was to be done at the hospital.

The outcome was that:

- the League was allowed to spay animals whose owners were unable to afford full veterinary fees;
- the League could enable homes to be found for any stray animals which were in the care of the hospital;
- immunisations could be carried out on animals admitted to the hospital, and on those whose owners could not afford full veterinary fees;
- no member of staff was to recommend any particular vet, and a full list of practising vets was to be compiled and made available for inspection by members of the public.

Another outcome of these discussions was the decision that in future the AVA should have a representative on the Board and this continued for several years. This seems to have eased the tensions between the two organisations. The first representative was Margaret (Peggy) Goodwin who joined in September 1967. She had previously worked at the hospital in the mid-1950s before going on to establish the largest veterinary practice in Ringwood. She was replaced in May 1969 by Dr Ruddock who, during the twelve months he remained on the Board, took a reasonably active role in the hospital's affairs.

In 1970 Alan Lawther was appointed as the AVA representative on the Board. The Board expressed some initial apprehension because Alan had returned to work part-time doing surgery at the hospital and they were reluctant to have a hospital employee as a member of the Board. However, their fears soon passed and when after two years Alan ceased to be the AVA representative he was asked to stay on in his own right. He remained a Board member until the mid-1980s. He was also employed by the Board at different periods to oversee the veterinary work of the hospital.

At the start of the 1980s the Victorian Veterinary Board began a series of assaults on the League. At first these were trivial and carping, but they became increasingly serious.

In August 1980 Dr Cimati was summoned to appear before the Victorian Veterinary Board charged with advertising the hospital's services. This resulted from an article in *The Sun* by Caroline Ross but Dr Cimati was able to convince the Board that its allegations were unfounded.

On 7 April 1981 the Veterinary Board complained about the wording of an advertisement in *The Age* for the sale of cats. To counter the criticism that the advertisement was promoting the hospital the wording was altered from the Lort Smith Hospital to the Animal Welfare League of Victoria.

In August 1981 the Veterinary Board complained that the League's advertisement in the Yellow Pages was too large.

In December it commenced legal action against the League over its employment of veterinary officers. The matter was resolved only with a change in legislation, the Veterinary Surgeons (Amendment) Bill, which passed through parliament in early 1983. This allowed a recognised body to provide a veterinary service, and allowed the Governor-in-Council to declare any body corporate or unincorporate to be a recognised body, provided that the principal object of the body was the promotion of the welfare of animals.

In February 1983 Mrs Kwiatek, secetary/manager, was instructed to apply for the Animal Welfare League to be declared a recognised body under the act.

This was not the end of the affair. In September 1984 the Veterinary Board of Victoria said that it would recommend that the League be declared a recognised body only if it gave an undertaking that it would provide for sick and injured animals, treatment which 'would be primarily concerned with stray and unwanted animals and for such stray and unwanted animals provide consultative and treatment facilities'. In other words the veterinary Board was asking the hospital to cease providing a treatment service to the general public, which, since there was no money to be made in treating strays, was the hospital's only direct source of revenue.

The matter was dealt with between the solicitors employed by the respective parties, and the Veterinary Board appears to have recognised the futility of this course of action because the issue was not pursued. The proclamation recognising the Animal Welfare League as a recognised body was finally made by the Governor-in-Council on 19 February 1985.

10 Treating the animals

The early hospital treated a number of horses. Such patients are not seen at the hospital today and the old stables which used to accommodate them have been demolished. In the 1930s horses were still an essential part of everyday business – milk carts, night carts (for sanitation) and the old rag-and-bone man were only a few of the trades that depended on horses for transport. As the depression deepened many of these businesses found it increasingly difficult to care for and treat their animals. Some were pushed beyond their strength and there were times when they had to be rescued by the League.

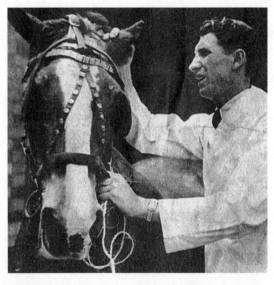

Mr Ron Greville treats a horse, *Unidentified newspaper,* *AWL scrapbook.*

The Australasian Journal of Pharmacy, 31 October 1931, included an article about the clinic, commending its work but particularly mentioning the generosity of Mrs Lort Smith:

Horses are a problem, those generally admitted being old and ill-conditioned. Frequently they are the means of livelihood of a poor dealer in bottles and bags. Often they are far beyond veterinary skill, and must be condemned as unfit for further work and subsequently destroyed by a humane 'killer'.

That the owner of the unfortunate horse thus condemned may not suffer the loss, the kind and sympathetic honorary secretary often buys the poor beast from him herself, though she knows it must be put out of its misery at once. Horses whose main need is good food and rest can, if their owners are willing, receive this at the Rest Home for Horses at Ashburton.

Probably the last time that a horse was treated at the Lort Smith was in the 1960s when Alan Lawther recalls treating maybe half a dozen, mainly children's ponies. There are no longer any facilities in which they could be treated now that the grass area has been built over.

Boy and horse at the old veterinary clinic,
Photo: Lort Smith Animal Hospital, AWL scrapbook.

Horses being treated at the Lort Smith Animal Hospital, *Photo: Lort Smith Animal Hospital, AWL scrapbook.*

One of the more unusual animals treated at the hospital was a camel from Melbourne Zoo. In 1975 the hospital rescued a family of ducks who had strayed from the Botanic Gardens into the Children's Court which was then situated in Batman Avenue.

A camel visits hospital, *Unidentified newspaper, AWL scrapbook.*

CAMEL VISITS HOSPITAL.—This camel, which is well known to children on Melbourne's beaches, was taken yesterday to the Animal Welfare League's Hospital for a nasal operation to enable him to be led about by a short rope

Ducks get a lesson in law,
The Sun, 17 October 1975,
AWL scrapbook.

Ducks get a lesson in law

By HEATHER WILLMAN

MOST mothers teach their children the difference between right and wrong at an early age.

And mother ducks are no exception.

Yesterday, a mother duck from the Botanic Gardens took her 11 ducklings across Batman Av., for a lesson in law.

She walked them through the open door of the Children's Court and up to the Magistrate's Bench.

Luckily the court was not in session.

When rescuers from the Lort Smith Animal Hospital arrived the ducks had made themselves at home underneath the bench.

Hospital manager Maureen Gallop said: "We came armed to the teeth with five cat cases, a net and a blanket.

"We thought they were holding up traffic in Batman Av."

The ducks led two ambulance drivers from the hospital and Miss Gallop a merry chase around the courtroom before they were eventually caught.

"The ducklings went everywhere, and it is not easy trying to catch them on a slippery vinyl floor," Miss Gallop said.

Mother Duck and her ducklings will be returned to the Botanic Gardens today, no worse off for their tangle with the law.

● DIANNE ROSS, 21, a kennel nurse at the animal hospital, looks after the mother duck and her ducklings.

Mrs Norman Welsh told the story at the 1947 annual general meeting of one of the hospital's more memorable and difficult patients, a snake imported to Australia to take part in a show at a local entertainment venue:

It was a very valuable snake sent from overseas to be used in a performance at the Tivoli. It became uncontrollable, but the owner wanted to keep it for its skin. He brought it to the hospital to be destroyed. The snake caused turmoil in the hospital, so it was put in the lethal chamber. There the gas had no effect. It just thrived on it. In the end the snake was destroyed by the surgeon, but it went away in its box still wriggling.

Alan Lawther recalls the pattern of pet ownership during the 1960s:

An increasing relative affluence brought an insatiable demand for dog ownership, and indiscriminate breeding resulted in deterioration of conformation and temperament in many breeds. Poor handling skills compounded this and it was common for dogs being brought for treatment to be unmanageable.

Cats were usually domestic but exotics were seen infrequently, and these were mostly Siamese, although toward the end of the decade the Burmese and Abyssinian began appearing. Sadly the cat had not yet attained the standing of the dog as a pet and tended to be neglected from a treatment point of view. Market and pet shops were able to provide a replacement for 20 cents (about $1.50 by today's prices). As a consultation would cost around $1, many cats had to take their chances. There were still some very devoted cat owners who were willing to try their utmost to retain their pet, no matter what. But having to put down so many cats was extremely stressful to the hospital staff.

The local population was mainly 'blue collar' and aged pensioners, with growing numbers of European migrants. These people had often experienced two world wars as well as the Great Depression. The majority had only the most basic education and their management of animals was often based on folklore. The seeking of veterinary attention was thus often delayed because of inability to recognise a problem in its early stages or a historical belief that animals were 'well able to look after themselves', or because of economic concerns.

The dogs which presented were mostly of the smaller breeds with terriers occupying a leading place. Pekingese, pugs and dachshunds were also common, with spaniels, setters and retrievers marking the upper end of the size range. Larger breeds were less common but as the decade progressed the German Shepherd became more popular due to migrant familiarity with them in Europe.

Two diseases were particularly prevalent at this time. In dogs distemper was the primary cause of loss of huge numbers of young animals as well as life-long debilitation in others. An effective vaccine became available in the late fifties replacing one which could have devastating side effects. A virulent dose of the disease was injected into one side of the dog's body,

Mrs Norman Welsh and a St Bernard dog, *Unidentified newspaper, AWL scrapbook.*

followed half an hour later by an antidote injected into the other side of the body. For a short period of time the vaccinated dog was more susceptible to the desease should it encounter distemper from another dog before the immunity had had the chance to fully develop. Some older dog owners retained vivid memories of healthly dogs having been vaccinated to prevent distemper but instead they contracted it. These people were loath to embrace the newer treatment and so the desease continued to wreak havoc. In cats feline enteritis was rampant, causing acutely rapid death in youngsters. The few that recovered appeared to have no long term effects. Again a vaccine became available but in this case, because of the standing of cats in society which has already been mentioned, few people used it.

Today both of these diseases have been almost completely eliminated and many vets today have never seen them. However, for those who lived through that period the memories of such cases and their emotional effect upon the associated humans burns fierce in memory. Sadly, as described earlier, the Australian Veterinary Association prevented the hospital using either vaccine. In retrospect this action was unconscionable.

The diet of pets in those days was mainly table scraps and offal. Some diseases were diet related: cats fed only on liver developed growths of excess bone while cats fed nothing but ox heart developed paper-like bones. Pet foods were introduced later and contributed to ending these problems.

The 1960s saw a great increase in the variety of drugs available for combating disease and the establishment of more scientific methods of investigating a clinical case. While the early years saw vets arriving at a diagnosis by use of their five senses and experience, the end saw much greater use of clinical pathology which was becoming more available to the profession.

Client education played a large part in this, both direct and by word of mouth. As anaesthetics were improved the risk in surgical procedures was reduced and owners were much readier to subject their pets to surgery.

Today the animals that are brought in for treatment are mainly family pets but birds and other wildlife are not uncommon.

Tiny Tim with Miss Heather Needs, *The Age*, June 1978.

Stray animals are often brought to the Lort Smith and attempts are made to locate their owners. The press has a major role in this, and is often successful in bringing about reunification as these two photographs, from *The Age* in June 1978, show.

It is not only dogs and cats who become lost. In June 1965 a lamb believed to have fallen from a transport truck in Bacchus Marsh, was brought to the hospital to be cared for and a home found.

Where a stray's owner cannot be found it may be rehomed or, if believed to be unsuitable for rehoming, it may be euthanased. The focus of the League had always been to eliminate animal suffering so it was consistent with its charter that the Board decided, in May 1931, that all animals should be given morphia before undergoing treatment or before they were destroyed. In 1936 the hospital had two lethal chambers. The

Mr Holandsjo and Tiny Tim, *The Age*, June 1978.

A cat being put into a lethal chamber, 1930s, *Unidentified newspaper, AWL scrapbook.*

one for dogs used carbon-monoxide, but chloroform was used for cats. In the 1940s non-veterinary staff were restricted to using the lethal chamber when no vet was on duty. Otherwise it was usual for vets to euthanase animals with a lethal injection.

In March 1969 the League was invited to a meeting organised by the RSPCA to discuss details of a new method of euthanasia called the Euthanair. A leaflet was obtained for the committee's information. This method was never taken up by the League which believed that lethal injections caused the animals less suffering, although they were more expensive. Both the RSPCA and the Lost Dogs' Home adopted an alternative form of euthanasia, the Lethanair, in the early 1970s. Both institutions suffered from negative publicity because this form of euthanasia was believed by the general public to cause pain and distress to the animals. The League was anxious that it should not be caught up in the negative sentiment and publicised the fact that it continued to put animals to sleep through lethal injection.

Hospital staff develop a great affection for and empathy with the animals in their care, so it is not surprising that the disposal of unwanted or unclaimed animals has been an on-going problem for the hospital. On occasions it has been reported to the Board that some vets had been unwilling to euthanase cats. Advances in veterinary treatment, as well as a greater recognition of the role which animals play in the community and the importance of animal welfare, has perhaps increased the pressures on veterinary staff. In earlier years animals that were euthanased had less likelihood of health and well-being than animals in a similar situation today.

Kittens have posed a particular problem for hospital staff, and the Board has occasionally had to clarify the rules so that the hospital was not overloaded. For instance in March 1991 there were thirty kittens in the cattery (the maximum number was supposed to be twelve) because of the refusal of some vets to put unwanted kittens to sleep. In February 1990 a veterinary nurse resigned due to the stress of dealing with euthanasia.

The League has always been totally opposed to research on animals, although there have been a few occasions on which it has agreed to donate organs from dead animals where there were clear gains to be made in human medicine. For instance in 1964 it agreed to co-operate with the Melbourne School of Veterinary Science over research on parasites by providing the school with samples of alimentary canals of cats and dogs put to sleep in the course of daily work.

Again in November 1966 the Board agreed to give the pancreases of dead cats to Monash University for research into the production of insulin in a study of diabetes in humans and animals. The scheme was to be trialled for six months on condition that no publicity be given to the matter.

In September 1971 it was agreed that dead puppies should be given to the Veterinary Research Institute for research into the herpes virus, with the proviso that 'discretion must be used'.

A request from a zoology student in February 1982 that she be allowed to examine the stomach contents of stray cats brought to the hospital was turned down on the basis that the Board did not have the right to allow it. No further explanation was given for the decision which was not consistent with earlier decisions.

In November 1988 the Board agreed that, subject to the views of the Cat Protection Society, healthy stray cats which would normally be put down should be given to the University of Melbourne Department of Ophthalmology to study the regenerative capacity of cat corneal endothelial cells in organ culture. This would be important for the study of certain types of corneal blindness in humans.

The hospital often has to find homes for stray or abandoned animals, and much care and thought goes into selecting the right homes. Where an animal has a special need, special care is taken. A good example of the lengths to which the staff may go is illustrated by the story of Eureka, a stray Dalmatian who was found to be deaf. A phone call was made to the Victorian Deaf Society (Vicdeaf) and through the work of Amanda Vlassis, a vet nurse, Eureka was linked up with Selwyn who was employed as a recreational officer in Vicdeaf's aged services area. Selwyn takes up the story:

A deaf Dalmatian! She seemed an appropriate companion as I had been searching the pet shops and papers for a pet for many months. It was appropriate to have a deaf puppy because the communication between a deaf person and deaf puppy is important. We have 'listening eyes' used in the sign language called Auslan.

Already my new christened puppy Eureka can pick 'sit', 'biscuit', 'toilet', 'sleep' (meaning good night), 'food' (meaning dinner time), 'good,' and 'bad' in the single vocabulary of Auslan. She will be taught other words. Eureka really loves and understands this communication.

Eureka enjoys many pleasures at home. She even has a 'green thumb', as she loves digging, rolling on the lawn, catching snails and even collecting snails and placing them under her mattress. By the time she has finished she has green paws.

Selwyn and Eureka, *Photo: Lort Smith Animal Hospital.*

It's not just the humans who help. Emma Mae is a German Shepherd/Malamute cross belonging to the caretakers Tom and Chris Farrell, and late one night she helped out by providing blood for an injured stray.

Emily Ensor was the winner of the New Zealand Veterinary Association Companion Animal Society/English Speaking Union Scholarship which is awarded every year. She spent time at the hospital in January 2002 and she gives an interesting view of the hospital:

The Lort Smith Animal Hospital was fascinating and I was very impressed with the facilities available. A nurse for every vet was a novelty – I had not observed that in NZ before. There is also such a large staff and different vets and nurses kept appearing every day that I was there!

I was particularly impressed with the Lort Smith's role in Animal Welfare in Melbourne, and especially the policy of de-sexing and tattooing the younger kittens and pups which were being rehomed ...

It was worthwhile spending two weeks in the hospital – especially because there are no clinics of comparable size anywhere in NZ. It also gave me a good insight into how urban small animal practice in Australia is different to New Zealand small animal practice in regards to the huge numbers of stray animals in Melbourne.

11 Community links

It was traditional for the wife of the Governor of Victoria to be the patron of the League – until recently she was always given the title of patroness. The tradition started with Lady Somers. Lord Somers left Melbourne in 1931 but he was not replaced until 1934 when Lord Huntingfield was appointed. Lord Dugan took over in 1939. Both Lady Huntingfield and Lady Dugan accepted the role of patroness.

Lady Dugan, *Animal Lover book of the Animal Welfare League,* 1940.

The tradition was broken with the next patroness. Lady Brooks, the wife of Sir Dallas Brooks who became Victoria's Governor in 1949, was invited to take on the role but turned down the offer, making the suggestion that her daughter, Miss Jeanette Brooks, who was about eighteen at the time, be asked to accept it in her place. On her acceptance Jeanette was invited to attend the annual general meeting on 12 April 1950, but the committee decided that the invitation was to 'intimate that she would not be expected to remain for the public meeting to follow, unless she so desired'. In fact she took her duties seriously: not only did Jeanette become the first patroness to attend an AGM, but she attended the following year also, having paid an informal visit to the hospital beforehand. Lady Brooks took over her daughter's role as patroness when, in 1953, Jeanette left Australia with her new husband Lieutenant Robin Byrne. Lady Brooks also agreed to be president of the Mrs Lort Smith Memorial Appeal which was launched in 1958, and Sir Dallas Brooks opened the new hospital extensions in May 1960. Lady Brooks accepted an invitation to become a life member of the League in 1979.

Lord Delacombe was appointed Victoria's Governor in 1963 and Lady Delacombe became patroness. She made two visits to the hospital, in August 1963 and on 29 November 1969 when she presented a mobile cot to the hospital on behalf of the junior members of the RSPCA.

In 1974 Mrs April Hamer, a friend of several Board members, took over the role of patron, thus breaking the long tradition of the wife of

Victoria's Goveror being invited to fill the position. She was the wife of Victoria's premier, Mr Rupert Hamer, whose government subsquently generously assisted animal welfare, particularly the Lort Smith Animal Hospital and the Lost Dogs' Home. Since the League's article of association only allowed for one patron these were changed to allow for two. In 1975 shortly after Sir Henry Winneke was appointed Governor, his wife, Lady Winneke, accepted the role of patroness.

In August 1982 Lady Murray, wife of Victoria's Governor, brought to the hospital for treatment an injured cat that had fallen two storeys from the roof of Government House. She was accompanied by her aide-de-camp in full uniform. She subsequently accepted an invitation to become a patroness. She was perhaps the patron who demonstrated the most interest in the activities of the hospital, and informed Sadie Howe in April 1983 that she wished to visit the hospital both before and after the kennel renovations. She made a visit in June 1983 and photos of the occasion were taken by Graham Cornish for the annual report.

Lady Murray officially opened the renovated hospital on 11 October 1984. She ceased her involvement with the hospital in 1985 when she left Melbourne but accepted life membership of the League.

In 1986 Mrs Jean McCaughey, wife of the next Governor of Victoria, accepted the position of patroness. She had been a local resident, and she wrote in her letter of acceptance that she had used the Lort Smith frequently. She visited the hospital in May 1986 to meet the staff, and on 24 September 1986 she handed over a new ambulance which had been bought with funds raised by the Essendon auxiliary. She resigned in March 1992.

Lady Delacombe, 1963, *Unidentified newspaper, AWL scrapbook.*

ALL he needs is love ... and Lady Murray, the Governor's wife, makes sure this 2½-month-old pup gets plenty of cuddles at the opening of the new extensions to the Lort Smith Animal Hospital yesterday. The little fellow, a German Shepherd cross, and his canine and feline mates at the hospital are looking for a good home.

Lady Murray, *The Sun* 12 October 1984, *AWL scrapbook.*

Lort Smith patrons Commodore Dacre Smyth and Mrs Jennifer Smyth at the launch of the new hospital, *Photo: Lort Smith Animal Hospital.*

Hospital patron Mrs McCaughey, with Mrs Phyl Taylor, Mrs Helen Allchin and Mrs Sadie Howe, *Photo: Norman Wodetzk.*

Commodore Dacre Smyth and his wife Jennifer were joint patrons from 1992 until their resignation at the start of 2002. Commodore Dacre Smyth was a painter and he generously donated seven of his works to the hospital. One of these was selected to print cards for the general use of the hospital.

Lady Marigold Southey AM, Victoria's Lieutenant-Governor and aunt of Samantha Baillieu, took on the role in 2002. She had previously been closely involved with the hospital through her position as president of the Myer Foundation.

The League was always keen for the University of Melbourne to re-open its Veterinary School, closed in 1929, because of the severe shortage of vets in Victoria. When the hospital had difficulty in recruiting a local vet the League frequently made contact with the

Universities of Sydney, Brisbane and even Edinburgh, but it was rare to get a positive response. The League twice approached the University of Melbourne, in 1948 and again in 1955. The first approach was made by letter to the vice-chancellor, and the response was discouraging, citing the high costs involved. The second was a direct approach to the vice-chancellor, Sir John Medley, by Mrs Lort Smith, and the reply in October 1955 was equally pessimistic. The cost of running such a school in Melbourne would be £375,000 and it would be cheaper to fund a scholarship for every Victorian student studying veterinary science interstate than to set up such a school. Undeterred, the Board persisted with its lobbying and wrote to the Premier and other politicians.

When the school did re-open in 1965 Dame Mabel Brookes met with Professor Blood to discuss the working relationship between the two institutions. The Professor said that he was 'delighted that students could attend the Hospital for practical experience (without payment, unless gainfully employed)'. Dame Mabel hoped that if they could come to a loose agreement the hospital's association with an educational institution might enable donations to be made tax deductible.

Lady Marigold Southey,
Photo: Courtesy of Government House.

Today the hospital enjoys close links with the University of Melbourne. Professor Ivan Caple, dean of the faculty of Veterinary Science, was the speaker at the 2001 annual general meeting. He traced some of the links between the hospital and the university. He had recently attended a forum at the Victorian Research Institute Library where he had met Will Chamberlain the last vet to graduate from the University of Melbourne when the Veterinary School closed in 1929. Will remembered being interviewed by Mrs Lort Smith for a job. He didn't get it because his experience was in research, and Mrs Lort Smith was very wary of this field of science.

Professor Caple pointed out that Louisa Lort Smith had been agitating for reforms which are still on the agenda today. Closer links between the hospital and the university had also been something which she and her successors Dame Mabel and Sadie Howe had pressed for. He then told the meeting that the two head veterinarians at the Lort Smith, Harold Pook and Patrick Cheah, were to be given the status of academic associates of the university which would enable them to supervise university students and also keep up to date in advances in veterinary science.

Pet therapy

Pet therapy for sick, elderly and handicapped people is a relatively new community concept, although most people with pets know very well how they can enhance health and happiness. In response to a request from the Little Sisters of the Poor nursing home, hospital supervisor Joan Sturzaker and ambulance driver Margaret Stevenson took some animals on a visit to the home in July 1984. The visit was very successful but a regular pet therapy program did not start until 1989. It continues to thrive under Joan's leadership, often with the assistance of Board members and volunteers, in particular Janet Clark and Denise Farmery. Elderly and infirm people are given the opportunity to interact with animals and this has a very positive effect on their sense of well-being. Joan describes her first visit to a nursing home in an early newsletter:

> *The very first visit I did was at the Mount Royal Nursing Home in Parkville. There was a man who had been in hospital for six months and never spoken with the exception of saying toilet and water. Upon putting a box containing a cat on his knee, the cat suddenly jumped out. To our surprise he said 'Oh how wonderful!' He became animated and started talking to me non-stop about how he walked his dogs along the river, and the names of his cats.*
>
> *As a consequence, nurses and doctors gathered around. Being my first visit I thought, what have I done wrong? They told me that he had never spoken before. There have been other examples similar to this story since. Quite often patients will want to walk a dog around the hospital. Wards and rooms liven up as a result. People would normally sit for hours in wheelchairs but now we have beautiful smiling faces as a result and many wonderful pet stories. The nursing staff have said how rewarding the visits are and, without exception, our future visits are eagerly anticipated by staff and patients alike.*

Mrs Olga Castleton of Ashley Terrace
Hostel nurses a kitten, October 2000,
Photo: Lort Smith Animal Hospital.

Bambi the lamb being fed by Jerry at Alton Court,
Photo: Lort Smith Animal Hospital.

Mrs Lorna Cannon of Hurlingham Day Centre with
Lambert, August 2000, *Photo: Lort Smith Animal Hospital.*

Pets are also taken to schools where students are taught how to relate to and care for animals. The pet therapy program is not a fundraising venture but it does bring in donations and assists in raising the profile of the hospital. Another benefit to the hospital was that the program attracted a grant from Tattersall's because it was directly targeting the care of people rather than simply animals. Continuing demand for the service after twelve years is a testament to its success.

One of the places which Joan visited was North Melbourne Day Care Centre for Senior Citizens. There, in February 1991, she was introduced to Mrs Annie Baker, who was born a few doors from the site of the present hospital in 1898. Annie had later moved to 16 Mary Street (which was owned by the hospital in the 1990s) before she moved into accommodation in Abbotsford Street. She had worked all her life in North Melbourne and retired from her job at the Bulla Cream factory at the age of eighty-six, after twenty-five years as the tea lady. The committee agreed that she should be invited to morning tea to meet the ladies of the committee. Annie died on 12 December 1999, only a few weeks short of having lived in three different centuries.

Mrs Annie Baker with Mrs Virginia Edwards,
Photo: Lort Smith Animal Hospital.

Fundraising

Fundraising has always been an integral part of the hospital's relations with the community. In 1946 Mrs Lort Smith bought a kiosk at the Melbourne Showgrounds for £100 to be used by the League during show week for publicity and fundraising. It required a good deal of maintenance every year and ground rent was paid to the Royal Agricultural Society. A roster of staff and Board members to operate the kiosk was prepared each year, and a pony or other animal was often on display to attract members of the public.

In 1982 the League was told that the kiosk's rental was to be raised from $95 to $800 and it was unable to renegotiate this amount. Although the League made a record profit of $1151 at the 1982 show the rental the following year was to be increased a

Miss Caroline Sturzaker with a Shetland pony at the showgrounds, 1970,
Photo: Courtesy of Joan Sturzaker.

further 10% and it decided to sell the kiosk back to the Royal Agricultural Society for $500.

Fundraising auxiliaries were introduced in the 1940s and continued to exist until the mid 1990s. The early ones existed in Black Rock and Ringwood and another was called the Raveloe group, but information about these is somewhat scant. More details are available about groups organised in more recent years.

The St Martin's group was formed from a number of animal lovers among the 'younger set' under the leadership of Joan Sturzaker. Starting in 1963 it raised substantial amounts of money. In November 1964 it donated £200 toward a new fridge and in 1966 it raised $4572. After the group disbanded Joan continued fundraising in her own right and in 1975 her projects raised $12,312.

The St George's group was run by Elizabeth Osborne and comprised mainly older people. It was less active than the St Martin's group and did not run for as many years. In 1966 it raised $1876.

Mrs David Bardas, Mrs Jim Watt and Mrs Ian (Joan) Sturzaker at a fundraising luncheon, 1964, *Photo: AWL scrapbook.*

Under the leadership of Pat Patience, the Brighton auxiliary was involved in making craft items for sale at the annual fete. Regular monthly meetings were held at the home of Sadie Howe, who provided lunch. Members swapped items which could be made into saleable goods. The 1989 newsletter particularly thanked Edna Walsh and her daughter who provided the auxiliary with an 'endless supply of beautiful dog coats. Also our friend Miss Pinkie Graham who is so generous in giving us lovely articles of handcraft to sell'. The Brighton auxiliary finally closed in February 1995 when Phyl Taylor and Pat Patience gave the balance of their fundraising activities to the Board in the form of a cheque for $609.

Mrs Gladys Smith, Mrs Sadie Howe, Lady Murray and driver
Mrs Margaret Stevenson celebrate the new ambulance,
Essendon Gazette, 15 June 1983, *AWL scrapbook*.

The Essendon auxiliary was a very active group of women started in the mid-1950s, under the leadership of its president Mrs Mills. In 1959 it was thanked for its gift of £212 and for twenty-eight dog coats. The auxiliary donated five blankets in July 1960, and in December 1962 the members specifically requested that the amount of £240 they had raised should be used for the crematorium. A further cheque for £400 was donated in 1963 which was specifically for the night service fund. The auxiliary operated throughout the 1960s but disbanded in 1974.

It was reconstituted in February 1978 by Mrs Gladys Smith (president) and Mrs Connie Hyland (secretary). Its membership in 1980 was fifty. It was again extremely active. Speakers were invited to regular monthly meetings, and a number of fundraising activities were held. These included a caravan in Puckle Street Moonee Ponds, which was a focus for street stalls and tin rattling; basket luncheons; and afternoon tea parties. The auxiliary was also involved in a campaign to bring in control of ownership and registration of cats, and regulation of the sale of domestic animals in pet shops.

In 1981 the Essendon auxiliary raised a little over $4000 toward a new ambulance for the hospital, and in February 1982 they held a very successful fashion parade. By 1983 they had raised $9500, and on 3 June 1983 the new ambulance was presented to the hospital by Lady Murray.

Their energies did not cease after these major efforts. In July 1983 they expressed an interest in building and operating a kiosk in the hospital grounds, and the hospital proceeded with the project. It was built on part of the old outdoor waiting bay. Whilst the work was proceeding they donated $835 for a new wet-dry vacuum cleaner for the kennel floors in 1984. The kiosk was opened on 7 September 1985, and made a profit of $1528 between that date and the end of the year. It was originally intended that this would be used by hospital clients, but in fact it was substantially used by staff and people who worked close by. The auxiliary also provided the kiosk with a fridge and an awning and during the same year they presented the hospital with a cryosurgery unit, which is used to freeze out cancerous tissue not easily removed surgically.

The new wet/dry vacuum cleaner in use in the kennels, *Photo: Norman Wodetski.*

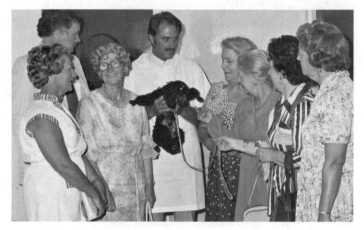

Essendon Auxiliary members with Dr Cimati and Mrs Sadie Howe. President, Mrs Gladys Smith is second from right, Mrs Connie Hyland third from right, *Photo: Norman Wodetski.*

The Essendon Auxiliary kiosk, *Photo: Norman Wodetski.*

Mrs Gladys Smith serving at the kiosk, *Photo: Norman Wodetski.*

Volunteer Mrs Thea Dickinson, *Photo: Lort Smith Animal Hospital.*

The kiosk, staffed by volunteers, made a profit of $6099 during 1986. Also during 1986 the auxiliary donated $3000 towards the cost of providing a covering for the dog-runs. The roofing covered half of the dog-runs, with louvres which could be closed in hot sun or rain.

Unfortunately a rift occurred between the auxiliary and the hospital. In 1987 Mrs Howe was told that the Essendon auxiliary had decided to change its name to the Friends of the Animals. The Lort Smith Hospital would continue to be the auxiliary's main charity but money would be directed to other organisations as it thought fit. The auxiliary also ceased to manage the kiosk.

Mrs Merna McGlaughlin took over the staffing of the kiosk, and a local pensioner lady was also employed during the week. Around the beginning of 1994 the Health Department brought in regulations requiring all food handlers to do a course and sit an exam, and this gave the Board an excuse to discontinue the employment of volunteers. The reason for the Board's wish to replace the volunteer service was related to insurance costs as well as the inconsistency of opening times. A decision was made to employ Tom and Chris Farrell on a salary to operate it from 10 am to 8 pm every day, initially on a two-month trial. Unfortunately many of the volunteers were upset by the way in which the changes were communicated to them; the Board agreed that the matter had been handled insensitively and made an apology.

Although the auxiliary officially closed in the late 1980s many of its members have remained stalwart supporters and fundraisers for the League. Mrs Gladys Smith was made a life member of the League in 1998. Mrs Merna McGlaughlin who joined the League in February 1981 was made a life member in 1994. Mrs Thea Dickinson continues to be an active supporter.

The North Melbourne Fair, now known as the Spring Fling, is an annual event which started in 1977. The Lort Smith Animal Hospital has had a fundraising stall at the fair since 1988, including a display of pet animals. This is co-ordinated by Joan Sturzaker. It not only raises money but also helps to enhance the profile of the hospital in the local community.

North and West Melbourne Community Festival, Spring Fling, 1997, Left to right: Ms Jillian Johnston, Mrs Joan Sturzaker, Mrs Virginia Edwards and Ms Janet Powell,
Photo: Lort Smith Animal Hospital.

Opportunity shops played a significant role in fundraising in the 1970s and 1980s. The League's first opportunity shop was opened in Richmond on 17 February 1970 under the leadership of Joan Sturzaker, and Dame Mabel Brookes held a cocktail party at her home, 'Elm Tree House', to launch the venture. Many well-to-do people were invited to attend and to donate the clothing they no longer wore. Dame Mabel commended the enterprise and said that opportunity shops, which were only recently being introduced, were the way to make money in the future.

Joan remembers working long hours in the opportunity shop with other volunteers. Mrs Gwen Adams, one of the older and more established Board members, used to warn the women that they should spend more time at home looking after their husbands or they would lose them – and they all did! Joan used to push her daughter

Caroline from South Yarra down Anderson Street and across the Morrell Bridge to the shop in Church Street, Richmond, with her little vinyl pram piled high with second-hand clothing. On the return trip up the steep hill it was laden with vegetables. Joan used to leave her big English pram at home because it was unsafe to push down the steep hill.

The shop was very successful, and one of its donations to the hospital was a public address system. For a while Joan had two shops going. Through the generosity of Betty Burstall who owned the La Mama Theatre she was able to rent the upstairs hall of the theatre in Carlton for the peppercorn rent of $2 a week. Joan also made generous personal donations to the League.

Another opportunity shop was bought in February 1977 in Johnston Street, Collingwood. It was a consistently profitable source of revenue for the League. A team of helpers included Virginia Edwards, Helen Durrant, Alison Lemon, Pam Bastow and Mrs Yencken. When Mrs Yencken, who was referred to as Auntie Hopie, died in 1987 her help was particularly missed.

The team had regular customers who often provided light relief and entertainment as this extract from the 1980 annual report demonstrates:

> We still have our regulars who are like old friends. One of our 'regulars' is a good looking woman who insists on telling us all her various love affairs in great detail! One of us disappears into the kitchen with the excuse that the kettle is boiling or some other urgent matter, leaving the other a captive audience! It's a case of 'The Quick and the Dead'. Some of our male customers even ask us out which is very flattering, but we always decline (nicely)!!

An extract in the annual report for 1981 by Helen Durrant and Virginia Edwards (who called themselves the Tuesday Girls) tells how one of the regular customers, believed to be in her fifties, surprised the staff by asking for maternity clothes, remarking that the baby was due on her fiancé's birthday. Today this would hardly be remarked on but then – 'Virginia could hardly believe it!' Then there was the Dancing King, a man no longer in the prime of his life who would be waiting for the shop to open to purchase frilly shirts. He reported that at dances he would have a queue of women waiting to partner him.

Plants regularly supplied by Pam Bastow and Marjorie Scott were a speciality of the Collingwood opportunity shop. Helen Durrant was a keen collector of dolls, which she dressed and sold for the League. She frequently appealed for donations of suitable dolls which were difficult to obtain.

The shop itself was in poor repair and needed a lot of maintenance. When it was sold in the late 1980s it was envisaged that another would be leased or bought but the costs involved, and the view that the energies of the volunteers could be better utilised elsewhere, led to this source of revenue being abandoned.

In past years there have been significant staff initiatives in fundraising. Four members of the Lort Smith staff took part in the Great Australian Bike Ride from Wangaratta to Melbourne between 2 and 19 December 1989. Mrs Tina Ward volunteered to make all the arrangements and she raised $1346 in sponsorship from businesses in North Melbourne. The local firm Wards Express was the most generous supporter, donating $850.

In September 1994 one of the staff members, Mark Inglis, organised a fundraising dance for the hospital which was also a social event for staff. The attitude of the Board to this generous move was very paternalistic. One Board member was concerned that the hospital's name would be brought into disrepute should anything go wrong, and perhaps to reassure her the secretary said that she would oversee the collection of money to ensure that the banking was done correctly. The Board was impressed that Mark paid for the invitations himself. Although it was hoped that it would become an annual event this did not occur. Mark resigned from his job in the kennels in October 1997.

Joan Sturzaker continues her tireless work in organising for volunteers to attend fundraising events at shopping centres, as well as continuing her pet therapy program.

In 1998 David White arranged for the English Speaking Union to establish two scholarship programs for students with an interest in veterinary studies to carry out work experience at the hospital for a period of two weeks to be funded by the ESU. One scholarship was established jointly with the New Zealand Veterinary Association Companion Animal Society, the other, known as the Kathleen Meagher Award, through the University of Adelaide.

The Lort Smith Animal Hospital has also been actively involved with the development of a program to encourage the care of dogs in an Aboriginal community in the Northern Territory. Dr Stephen Cutter was a part-time vet at the Lort Smith in the late 1990s. In 1997 he started a program providing a veterinary service in remote areas where his father was for many years in charge of the Aboriginal Health Services. Initially he travelled to the Northern Territory from Melbourne but subsequently bought his own practice in Palmerston. Two of the hospital nurses, Michael Curry and Steven Isaacs, travelled to the Northern Territory for a few months on different occasions to help Stephen deliver this innovative program. Their salaries were paid by the Board.

Due to the isolation and poverty of the communities they had rarely received veterinary attention before. Most of the dogs were virtually hairless, suffering from malnutrition as well as chronic mange and many other diseases. Their average life expectancy was only about three years as opposed to ten to twelve for the average Melbourne dog. One of the most important services which Stephen provided was desexing which not only reduced the number of dogs by about half but also made the dogs easier to care for as pets. The problem of dogs wandering off and fighting was reduced and there was more food to go around. Diseases such as heartworm, mange, ticks, lice and fleas were routinely controlled as part of the program. This means that not only has animal welfare improved but so have the social conditions of the communities concerned.

Stephen was careful to show his respect for the Aboriginal culture and to involve the communities in all decision making. He also trained local people in the skills necessary to continue the treatment of their animals. The program still continues, although Stephen has been able to obtain alternative funding and now relies less on the Lort Smith for assistance. Stephen Cutter was the guest speaker at the League's annual general meeting in March 1999.

Dog treatment in the in Northern Territory,
Photo: Mr Steven Isaacs.

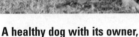

A healthy dog with its owner,
Photo: Mr Steven Isaacs.

Many individuals have provided the hospital with gifts and services. In February 1982 Margaret Stevenson, senior ambulance driver, was nominated for the North Melbourne Rotary Community Services Award. She had shown great determination and dedication to her job when she successfully rescued a dog which had fallen off a roof in Coburg. The job had taken four hours, with onlookers criticising her; finally she was helped by a man to whom she offered a dozen bottles of beer to climb onto the roof and drop a rope down to where she could attach it to the dog's leg and drag him free.

In 1978 she had been commended by the Board for her courage in collecting a savage stray cat which was suffering from an eye abscess.

The 1981 newsletter was produced by Dr Joan Humphreys who had given up veterinary practice for a while to become a court stenographer. She provided the materials and organised its printing. This newsletter was evidently well received because in December Miss Jean Wallan of Western Australia sent a donation of $60 in appreciation. Dr Humphreys continued to help the hospital by doing emergency sessions in times of staff shortage and by holding regular

Dog freed from his terror trap

Every dog has his day, and yesterday certainly was this dog's.

He fell off a roof at Coburg and became wedged, upside down in the 17 cm space between two houses.

But for the dedication of animal rescue worker Margaret Stevenson, he would have died there.

The dog was wedged so tightly, she couldn't pull him out — and the only humane solution, police at first thought, was to shoot him.

Miss Stevenson, however, would not give up. No one else would help, apart from onlookers who told her she was "doing it all wrong".

After four hours, a man agreed to help because Miss Stevenson offered him a dozen bottles of beer.

He climbed onto the roof, dropped a rope which Miss Stevenson tied around the dog — and finally he was freed.

Miss Stevenson is pictured with the dog — now named Tobby — at the Lort Smith Animal Hospital.

spaying clinics, and she also gave a talk to the Board on acupuncture in September 1981. In June 1982 she wrote a pamphlet on 'Care of your desexed pet after surgery' which was given to clients who had had their animals operated on at the hospital.

The annual general meeting on 18 June 2002 featured Dr Judith Slocombe as the guest speaker. Judith had worked as a locum vet during the first five years of the 1990s doing evening and weekend work. She had almost never missed a Saturday night shift during these five years as she worked to bring up nine children and start her own veterinary pathology business, initially working from home. Judith's business was highly successful and finally became incorporated into Gribbles (Pathology).

Saturday night was known as the 'graveyard' shift because it was not only extremely busy but dealt with many difficult and demanding crises. Judith spoke of the great experience which this work provided in teaching her to set priorities.

A retail shop situated in the reception area of the new hospital, for which the drug company Lyppard contributed the cost of the shelving, was opened in August 2001. It is staffed entirely by volunteers who are rostered by volunteer Narelle Clark. Volunteers have also continued to support Joan Sturzaker in her other promotional and fundraising activities at local shopping centres and other venues.

Ambulance driver Mrs Margaret Stevenson with a rescued dog, *The Age*, 9 June, 1979, *AWL scrapbook*.

Merlyn and Ron Brown until recently owned a printing shop around the corner from the hospital in Vale Street and for many years printed the hospital newsletters. They have been generous supporters of the hospital for thirty years, providing many acts of kindness. Merlyn is a frequent visitor to the hospital and is considered one of the Lort Smith 'family'.

As a result of viewing the ABC television documentary 'The Loved Ones' another Melbourne printer, Frank Wood of PAGE Pty Ltd. donated his services to design and produce four issues of the Lort Smith newsletter.

Richard Butterworth was a great lover of animals, cats in particular. 'The Loved Ones' featured Richard and his specially designed cat-a-lac, a cage on wheels, bringing cats and kittens to and from the hospital. He was filmed at home with his niece looking after twenty or so kittens which he reared on behalf of the hospital until they were old enough to be found homes. An architect, he was the only person to win the Gold Medal of the Royal Australian Institute of Architects for his specialist field of administration. He was an eccentric character and to quote from an obituary written by Jim Brady in the *North Melbourne News* (June 2000) after his death in May 2000:

His concern, however, was not limited to animals and he was a key person in the establishment of a Baptist children's home in Parkville which developed into a significant welfare agency now employing over 50 people.

With his long legs, thin body and high-pitched voice Richard did not project an image of great physical strength, but beneath the seemingly fragile frame there resided a rare strength of character along with a sharp mind and a wry sense of humour. He delighted in the description of himself as 'old and grey, bent and bony'.

Former colleagues and others who served with him on committees paid tribute to his ability to reduce messy detail to clear decisions and to produce concise minutes from wordy meetings. Richard's comment on this ... 'the one who takes minutes makes the decisions and the minutes should express what the committee wish they had decided'. Finally he always wrote with his pad on his high bony knees below table level because 'to let the windbags see you writing while they are speaking only encourages them to continue'.

Photo of Mr Richard Butterworth with his 'cat-a-lac', *Photo: Lort Smith Animal Hospital.*

In August 2000 Shirley and Len Lamb donated $20,000 which had been left to them in a will, to cover the expenses of setting up a website giving access to the public about the lost and stray animals being held at the hospital. Shirley Lamb and her friend June Peters have also been very vigilant in collecting stray cats from metropolitan Melbourne and bringing them in to be rehomed or destroyed. Shirley was made a life member of the hospital in 2000. Her mother, Edie Ruff, who used to live in North Melbourne, had also been extremely involved in the rescue of stray cats and kittens, most often on her own and using public transport. In her latter years, before she went to live in a retirement home, she spent a lot of time at the Lort Smith Animal Hospital assembling cardboard cat boxes which were sold to hospital clients – she loved talking to people and considered the hospital as her second home.

Volunteer Mrs Shirley Lamb with Dr Alan Lawther, *Photo: Lort Smith Animal Hospital.*

Also in August 2000 Colin McGennisken, a welder, offered to donate his expertise to the Lort Smith. He and a team of four volunteers made, dipped and covered with plastic inserts thirty-three beds which were worth between $120 and $150 each, making a total in-kind contribution of their work between $4000 and $5000.

Staff at the hospital have also shown great understanding and compassion toward clients, helping out the sick and needy whenever possible. One of the administrative workers received a phone call from a hospital on AFL Grand Final day to say that a patient who was a longstanding client of the Lort Smith was worried about leaving her dog alone and asking if Jeannie McKenzie, who knew her well, would look after it. Jeannie had no access to a key, so had to climb over a rickety fence to get in to collect the dog, and climb back over with the dog. She was chuckling to herself as she did so, wondering what all the drivers going past must be thinking, but also reckoning that they would be too concerned about the Grand Final to care very much. This patient had several prolonged periods in Royal Park Hospital, and Jeannie and Joan Sturzaker used to visit her there.

When the Lort Smith was contacted by a psychiatrist at the Royal Melbourne Hospital concerning a patient who had a phobia about dogs, and whose young daughter was developing the same phobia,

Mrs Joan Sturzaker and volunteer Mrs Edie Ruff, *Photo: Lort Smith Animal Hospital.*

Jeannie McKenzie took one of the hospital dogs to several sessions at the hospital, and she observed the patient and her daughter making progress during the time she attended.

Chris Farrell, hospital caretaker, was also approached by her GP to assist a Japanese lady with a phobia about big dogs, and the lady used to accompany Chris and her large dog on their walks until she had overcome her anxieties.

Anna Huntley was a staff member who died from a heart attack in 1996. She was passionate about wildlife and spent a great deal of her own time taking sick and orphaned wildlife to specialised care facilities. Her family donated $50,000 in her memory, which they had received from her superannuation fund. The staff, as a memento to her, made a collection which was used to manufacture possum houses for sale.

The Board was keen to use the latest technology to promote itself, and in 1998 it supported the introduction of an internet site to enable the

The late Ms Anna Huntley, *Photo: Lort Smith Animal Hospital.*

Mrs Jeanie McKenzie, Administration Supervisor, *Photo: Lort Smith Animal Hospital.*

hospital to advertise on a worldwide basis. The website was developed and maintained by hospital vet Dr Fiona Anderson.

Individuals who have assisted the hospital in myriad ways are too numerous for each name to be recorded here. A representative few, mainly from the later years of the hospital, have been mentioned in this chapter.

12 The campaign trail

Under the terms of its charter the Animal Welfare League has been consistently campaigning for changes in legislation and animal practices throughout the seventy-two years of its existence. Educating the public about the needs of animals has always been a priority. This education has been targeted at different groups – pet owners, owners of animals used for industrial purposes and people concerned with the care and management of animals in the wild.

For the first twenty-five years the League was directly involved in campaigning, but since the mid-1950s its approach has been less direct as it has concentrated its time and energy on running the hospital. The change may also be related to the passing of some of the more stalwart campaigners, but it is also important to realise that many of the League's aims had been achieved by this time as the more institutionalised and blatant forms of abuse had largely been eradicated.

Nevertheless the League has continued to initiate moves and to support other bodies in promoting the needs of even the most humble of animals, and those whose needs can be easily overlooked. For example in September 2001 Dr Alan Lawther wrote to the secretary of an agricultural show about the plight of fish sold to children in plastic bags and suggesting that they be sold in more suitable containers with an accompanying leaflet on how to care for the fish:

> Agricultural shows are an affirmation of our appreciation and respect for the land and the domesticated animals with which we have developed extremely strong bonds.
>
> A cornerstone of this bond is the implicit belief that we are the guardians of not only the species we proudly accompany at such events, but also any living creature that comes within our domain.
>
> Almost invariably the purchaser was a delighted youngster who proceeded home with his new pet visibly swimming around in a carefully tied clear plastic bag. Unfortunately most of these creatures would be dead by the time the new owner arrived home. The youngster would no doubt recover from his grief, but for the fish the distressful suffocation was mortal and permanent ...

In the late 1920s cars and trucks had only partially replaced more basic means of transport, and animals were commonly used as beasts of burden. Infirm and elderly horses were often seen pulling carts in the streets. Legislation to ensure that these animals were properly fed and housed was inadequate. Transport of animals to slaughterhouses, and slaughtering methods once they arrived there, were two of the issues in which the Animal Welfare League became involved. During the depression years the men who relied on their horses to obtain their livelihood were themselves suffering the effects of poverty and the competition for business could be cut-throat. There is one report of a man allegedly having three of his horses poisoned by a competitor.

In May 1933 Mrs Lort Smith represented the League in an interview with the Victorian Chief Secretary, Mr McFarlane, to try to obtain more protective legislation for animals and birds. She reported to the Board that she had been given a sympathetic hearing, and she was asked to send details of suggested new clauses. The Board responded that they thought only two clauses were necessary: giving authorities the power to prosecute cases of suspected animal cruelty; and giving them the power to destroy unwanted animals. As a result of the legislation the League was able to employ inspectors to investigate animal cruelty.

Mrs Lort Smith later asked for more changes to the proposed legislation, with the following suggestions:

- The sale of unfit horses should be prohibited, and the penalty for working sick horses should be more drastic. She gave England as an example of enlightened legislation: if a person had three convictions against him for cruelty to a horse, the animal could be taken from him.
- Greater control over the keeping of animals. The League had received numerous complaints that country people were keeping dogs chained up and horses tethered, often under the hot sun, and sometimes with no opportunity for exercise.
- She also directed attention to pigeon shooting and enclosed coursing which she suggested should be abolished. 'Men who had to amuse themselves by shooting at birds should take up golf or some other form of sport'.

- Regulation of the sale of puppies. Because of the harsh economic climate people were attempting to derive an income through the 'promiscuous breeding' of dogs. They tried to make a profit by selling the puppies, and many half-nourished animals were to be seen for sale at the markets.
- The training of animals for show purposes should be controlled.
- The sale of unweaned calves for meat should be disallowed.
- The indiscriminate sale of poisons for the destruction of animals should be stopped.
- The plight of Quamby's 3000 kangaroos was also brought to the attention of the government, with Mrs Lort Smith suggesting that the settlers upon whose land the kangaroos lived should not be responsible for them. 'If the kangaroos could be transported to a sanctuary so much the better, but if it were necessary to destroy them it was most undesirable that there should be a spectacular round-up. They should be shot expeditiously'.

The improper treatment of poultry was also alleged by Mrs Lort Smith at this time.

Another money making venture at this time was the stealing of cats for their skins. The *Herald* (28 August 1933) quoted Mrs Lort Smith saying that the League was to fight against the practice:

It is shocking to think that pet cats used to a home should be slaughtered for their skins, said the directress. (We have just taken the first step in the campaign by asking the police to find out where the skins are taken and sold.)

I have had many complaints recently that cats have been stolen. Regular sales in the city of cat skins encourage that sort of thing ... Only yesterday I had a complaint from a bank manager's wife in North Melbourne that her valuable cat had been stolen. A man was seen to take the cat from a wall and put it in a bag.

The League also took every possible opportunity to provide the general public with educational material. Members wrote frequently to the papers reminding people to care for their pets when they went on holidays. Mrs Lort Smith wrote in 1932 promising to supply a list of people who would take care of them for a small sum. She also urged people not to carry dogs on running boards as this frequently caused pneumonia and rheumatism.

Some useful hints to dog owners were given in a circular issued by the Animal Welfare League in the *Herald* on 7 September 1933. An extract of the article says:

The circular urges that only raw meat be fed to dogs. It is their natural food. Paraffin oil is recommended as superior to castor oil for all bowel trouble.

Too frequent washing is bad for a dog. The best thing is to keep its coat well brushed and sprinkled with insecticide.

A warning was given against the danger of distemper infection, of which the general symptoms were lassitude, loss of appetite, feverishness and a hot, dry nose. And if you had any suspicions in regard to internal parasites, 'grated carrots are given as a certain cure for worms'.

The League sometimes became involved in assisting animals which were suffering through epidemics or natural disasters such as bushfires. In the early 1930s there was severe hardship amongst farmers in the Mallee as drought and disease struck. Many were unable to afford veterinary treatment for their livestock. The VSPA was itself struggling for funding and appealed at a meeting for funds to allow a vet in Ballarat, Colonel A. Callow, to tour the area and provide as much help as he could. Mrs Lort Smith immediately gave a generous subscription herself and advertised in the press under the name of the Animal Welfare League. The appeal raised about £100. On 29 January 1930 the committee also decided to pay to graze six starving Mallee horses at the VSPA's Rest Home for Horses at a cost of 3/6 per week each.

Colonel Callow found dreadful conditions amongst the farmers, whose work came to a standstill if one of their ploughing team was disabled. He found an epidemic of strangles, a very contagious bacterial infection of horses. Treatment today is through antibiotics which were not available in those days. Equine influenza, cancer, shoulder sores, ulcers and acute tooth trouble were also prevalent. He found some horses with open wounds the size of saucepans. One horse was still tethered to the plough, though its skull had been eaten away to the brain by a cancer.

Unfortunately after making two trips to the region, and when he was all prepared for his third visit, Colonel Callow died. Mrs Lort Smith wrote to the Veterinary Society hoping to find a successor. In 1935 the district Returned Services League and the VSPA organised the farmers of the Mallee so that they could make the most of vets visiting that area.

A combined meeting of various organisations held in November 1933 discussed the fact that there were thousands of starving, mangy and emaciated cats in Melbourne that should be humanely put out of their misery. A campaign was organised by a group of representatives from the League, the Ornithologists Society, the Zoological Gardens, the Field Naturalists' Society and the Society for the Prevention of Cruelty to Animals that was to be conducted by the League. An anonymous gift of an ambulance had been made to the League to enable it to collect stray cats from around the city. Unfortunately the campaign did not eventuate because of the high cost of the chloroform required for their painless destruction. A competition was held to design a cat trap which could be manufactured for the League, and about eighty designs were received.

The Melbourne Zoo became the focus of public attention in the mid-1930s and the Animal Welfare League took a role in promoting a change in conditions. It publicised the case of a parrot which had such an overgrown beak that it could not eat and had to be destroyed. Wombats were kept exposed to the heat in narrow cages with concrete floors, whereas they naturally sought seclusion in burrows.

Entries in the competition for humane cat traps, *Herald* **c1933,** *AWL scrapbook.*

The centenary of the foundation of Victoria was celebrated in 1934, and many events were planned, including a rodeo to be called the Wild Australia Stampede to be held at Olympic Park in October and November. Mima Andrew, vice-president, wrote letters to *The Sun* on 5 February suggesting that the organisers confer with animal welfare bodies to ensure that the animals were not subjected to cruelty. Mrs Lort Smith followed this letter up the next day with another making the same suggestion but specifying the Animal Welfare League as the organisation that should be consulted. The issue of the rodeo polarised the Melbourne community but succeeded in uniting all the churches in their condemnation. Much was made of the fact that the British parliament was in the process of passing legislation which would ban rodeos in the United Kingdom and there was a lot of concern expressed that the Australian culture would be seen by overseas visitors as barbaric and lacking in sophistication. However, the rodeo was strongly supported by the Melbourne City Council under the leadership of the Lord Mayor, Sir Harold Gengoult Smith, the son-in-law of Dame Mabel Brookes. Despite sustained opposition the rodeo went ahead, but not without some difficulty caused by adverse weather conditions. Mrs Lort Smith was thanked by the management of the Wild Australian Stampede for the assistance she and members of the League had provided in caring for the horses and cattle used in the show, and she was assured of their cooperation in the welfare of the animals. She was offered free entry to all events but it is not known if she attended.

LONG-HORNED BULLOCKS are occasionally jammed in the race at Wangaratta trucking yards, and injury to the animals results. One seen in the foreground is being gored by another following. Worse happens in the trucks, in which the bullocks spend almost 12 hours on the trip to Melbourne. Those shown fetched 12 guineas each at Newmarket.

Long horned bullocks being loaded in the race at Wangaratta cattle yards, *The Sun*, **27 March 1934,** *AWL scrapbook.*

On 28 March 1934 a joint letter from Mr Ryan, the League's secretary, and Mrs Lort Smith appeared in *The Sun*. It commented on a photograph that had appeared in that newspaper showing long-horned bullocks jammed in the race at Wangaratta trucking yards. Once loaded on trucks or trains the bullocks spent twelve hours on their journey to Melbourne. Both these procedures resulted in frequent injuries. The letter suggested that the stock races be widened and partitions be erected in the trucks to prevent this. The consequent rise in freight charges would be offset by the fewer injuries incurred.

The politician Sir Henry Gullett told the 1934 annual general meeting of the League that he:

blamed the inventive engineer for the fact that we are still trucking animals by the same methods as years ago. Present facilities are as crude and as rough as when I was a little boy. It is time that trucking methods were improved. I would not be a party to imposing even a farthing increase on transport costs, but, as we are largely a pastoral people, we should show a deep interest in our animals.

New ramps for unloading sheep from trucks, *The Sun*, 2 April 1935, *AWL scrapbook.*

At the same meeting Lady Fairbairn said that attempts had failed to secure legislation to deal effectively with people who ill-treated their animals. She gave as an example the case of a dog which had been chained to one kennel for nearly thirteen years and was now living in a hole dug at the side of the kennel. It had hardly been allowed off the chain, and its only food had been a piece of meat thrown to it each day. The owner could not be prosecuted because the dog had been regularly fed each day.

The League employed an inspector who patrolled the stock saleyards, often accompanied by some of the League members. On 16 October 1934 Mrs Lort Smith and Mr Ryan described some of their observations in a letter to *The Argus*:

Sheep and lambs have fallen down and could not get up again. They were either dead or had sustained serious injury. The methods of unloading call for reform. It is a common sight to see lambs and sheep picked up by the wool and thrown over the side of the truck to the ground.

Lady Fairbairn, in her capacity as president of the Animal Welfare League, also wrote to *The Argus* (3 March 1935) to oppose the relocation of the Newmarket saleyards. She suggested that better planning and improvements in the layout and conditions of the yards would greatly enhance the care the animals received. One positive outcome was the introduction of better designed unloading ramps. They were wider and had side rails to prevent sheep jumping or falling off. In August 1935 a royal commission was set up into the running of the Newmarket saleyards, with the particular brief of recommending whether or not the yards should be relocated. Lady Fairbairn gave evidence and repeated her view that the yards should remain but should be upgraded to provide livestock with suitable conditions.

Lady Fairbairn giving evidence to the Saleyards Commission, 1935, the *Herald*, 2 August 1935, Newspaper Collection, State Library of Victoria.

Although the efforts of the League, led mainly by Mrs Lort Smith, to bring about reforms continued to a certain extent during the Second World War, once the war was over Mrs Lort Smith began to fight with renewed vigour for reform of some of the wider aspects of animal welfare. On 23 August 1947 she travelled to Canberra where she petitioned Mr McKell, the Governor-General. Among the issues she discussed were:

• better transport by road and rail for animals
• setting-up of inland killing centres
• use of captive bolt pistols in all Australian slaughterhouses
• abolition of the casting pen in the Jewish kosher killings
• no killing of immature calves
• registration of all riding schools
• banning of the continual chaining of dogs.

The Reverend L. L. Elliot and Mrs Hills, speakers at the Anti-Cruelty Campaign meeting, June 1950, *Unidentified newspaper, AWL scrapbook*

After the war the University of Melbourne asked local municipal councils to provide it with access to stray dogs and many, including Melbourne City Council, agreed. Mrs Doris Bray was a member of the Animal Welfare League and also a columnist with *The Sun*. Writing as 'Prudence' she took up the cause of dog owners who protested against the decision, and also challenged the basis of the ruling that a dog unclaimed after forty-eight hours should be sold. In her column on 14 December 1946 she quoted a letter from a widow with a sad tale:

> *I am a lonely old woman. I was recovering from the shock of my husband's death when my sole remaining companion, my little dog, disappeared. Someone must have left the gate open while I was lying ill. Nearly a week later a friend told me she had seen him taken by the dog cart.*
>
> *Through the unavoidable delay in making inquiries I never saw him again. This happened nearly two years ago and I still fret over his possible fate. I shall always believe that he went out looking for my husband, as he was his constant companion.*

Legislation was later passed extending the time a lost dog should be held before it was destroyed.

'Prudence' also asked for an assurance that there was no truth in the reports that dogs used for experiments had their vocal cords severed so that they could not make a sound. On 17 December 1946, R. Douglas Wright, Professor of Physiology at the University of Melbourne, replied:

I agree with many of the things she [Prudence] says and can well imagine her horror at the thought of the dogs losing their vocal cords. It is not a practice in Melbourne to injure the vocal cords of the dogs. Prudence does, however, appear to overlook the fact that even the institutions run by people most vocal in their good will to dogs do destroy large numbers of dogs. I know that they find homes for some strays, but they do kill a large number. I am only asking that these dogs which are to be killed should be killed just as humanely for research purposes.

Mrs Lort Smith wrote to *The Argus* on 4 January 1947:

Sir: The council and hundreds of members of the Animal Welfare League of Victoria are greatly disturbed by the decision of many municipalities to hand over collections of dogs in streets to the University for research. These collections may include hundreds of dogs, and surely all are not required. What becomes of the residue? I realise that animals (unfortunately) must be used, but discrimination should also be a factor, and the dog eliminated from research work as much as possible.

Initiating an anti-cruelty campaign, the League called an extraordinary meeting in January 1950 in response to disclosures made by the *Herald* of the appalling and barbaric cruelty existing in the various industries connected with transport and sale of animals being slaughtered for human consumption. It went on to organise a public meeting, to be held in the Lower Melbourne Town Hall on Monday 15 January at 8 pm. The sub-committee to help with the arrangements was made up of Lady Brookes, Mrs Lort Smith, Mrs Welsh, Mrs Read, Mr Watt, the Reverend Courtnay Thomas and Mr Ross Grant.

As a result the Animal Welfare League Anti-Cruelty Campaign was founded. Many religious leaders were prominent in the movement. The committee was made up of:

Members of the League; Mr G. Crowther, Mr C. M. Watt, the Reverend Courtnay Thomas, Lady Brookes, Mrs Lort Smith meet with the Chief Secretary over cruelty to animals, February 1950, *Unidentified newspaper, AWL scrapbook.*

Chairman	Rev. L. L. Elliot, a vicar from North Fitzroy
Vice-Chairman	Rev. W. J. Salter
Hon. Organising Secretary	Miss J. Richmond
Hon. Secretary	Miss J. Simmons
Hon. Treasurer	Rev. Courtnay Thomas
Committee:	Father F. K. Brennan, Major K. Downing, Mrs N. Welch, Mrs Lort Smith, Mrs C. Trathan, Mrs Warne Smith, Mrs G. Edwards, Mrs E. Onslow, Mr C. M. Watt, Miss M. Foley, Mr L. W. Anderson

By 1951 the League was able to report excellent progress in its campaign to introduce the use of the captive bolt pistol. It had collected 60,000 signatures from the public and was also researching the factors which were inhibiting change. The main one was the cost of providing specially designed pens with clamps to hold the animals' heads while they were being killed, and the additional costs associated with the redesign of abattoirs. The League had extensive discussions with the British Trade Commissioner regarding the design and manufacture of pens made in the UK, but it subsequently learnt from the only specialist in manufacturing pens in Australia that the type of clamp used in England was unsuitable in many Australian situations because animals here were not as docile as the stall-fed English stock.

The League also had discussions with two slaughtering firms in Melbourne, Borthwick & Sons, and Norman Smorgon & Sons. These were using the captive bolt pistol with complete success without any equipment other than the standard pen. They slaughtered the animals by shooting them in the head from behind, so no clamp was needed.

First the industry and the public had to be convinced that this method was painless and effective. The Anti-Cruelty League enlisted the help of two other churchmen, the Reverend L. I. Perkins, associate secretary of the Council of Churches, and Senior Major Southwell of the Salvation Army, and two representatives of primary producer associations, James Bryant and Alan Brownlee, to report on the suitability of the captive bolt pistol in slaughtering animals. They 'all stated that death by this method was absolutely instantaneous and painless, and they were astonished at the simplicity of the arrangements'.

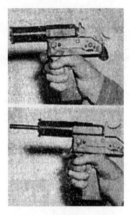

The captive bolt pistol,
Unidentified newspaper,
AWL scrapbook.

The next barrier was to challenge the commonly held view that the introduction of the captive bolt pistol would require expensive renovations to slaughterhouses. When, in December 1951, a question was asked in parliament as to whether steps would be taken to make the use of the captive bolt pistol compulsory the reply from the Minister of Health was that it would be too costly. The chairman of the Health Commission, Dr Cole, was interviewed on the radio and he continued to push this line. The League challenged him to produce an existing pen in which the captive bolt pistol could not be used, and when he failed to take up the challenge the Health Commission agreed to take a more open-minded approach.

Although the information about the method of safe use of the pistol had been available for fifteen years, no one had used that information in a constructive way to further the cause. It had taken a thirty-year fight before the Battle of the Bolt was finally won.

Another cruelty issue addressed by the Anti-Cruelty League was the inhumane treatment of drovers' dogs at the Newmarket saleyards. They found that the dogs were provided with inadequate food and shelter:

*Some of the dogs were tied with short pieces of wire which would not
allow them to lie down, all were on bluestone without any bedding, many
were without water, and so few tins could be found that it was some time
before we were able to give them all a drink. They were ravenously
hungry; we took with us a large suitcase of horse meat, prepared dog food,
and bread – four days old. The dogs went frantic as we fed them, and
after all the meat was finished, they ate the bread in the same desperate
way until nothing remained.*

One dog had recently given birth to a litter of stillborn puppies and
was in very poor condition. Her owner thought that someone had
kicked her and he no longer wanted her. She was taken to the Lort
Smith for treatment but could not be saved.

In December 1950 the government had passed amendments to the
Police Offences Act that provided penalties for people who set up
animals to be killed by dogs, or permitted any animal in captivity to be
injured or killed by a dog. This legislation was largely the result of
lobbying by the League. Unfortunately the legislation alone did not
prevent such cruelty happening – there was a problem with enforcement.

In March 1951 residents of Tottenham reported to the Anti-Cruelty
League that live cats, rabbits and possums were being used for
'blooding' greyhounds at White City trials. Both the *Herald* and the
League became involved in investigating the issue, and on 2 April the
Herald reported that:

*At least 19 live rabbits were thrown to greyhounds and killed – many
torn to pieces-during trials at the White City coursing track, Tottenham,
last night ... I saw rabbits with broken legs thrown to the greyhounds and
torn apart ... The 'pacer' was released before the dogs competing in the
trial. When the trial finished, the 'pacer' ran into an enclosure. The gate
was slammed on the competing dogs. Inside the enclosure a rabbit was
thrown to the 'pacer'. Trainers said that the 'pacer' was allowed to kill a
rabbit to encourage it to run faster in succeeding trials. Other dogs were
given live rabbits for 'kills' after they had raced. I was told that the dogs
liked to hear the rabbits squeal when they died.*

As a result of the publicity a police investigation was ordered by the
Chief Secretary, and his office notified clubs that, in the event of

rabbits or other game being found to have been used on their tracks, their licences would be cancelled forthwith. The Victorian Council of Greyhound Racing also took a strong line against the practice and promised to take steps to enforce the legislation.

The League also revisited the issue of cruelty to animals in saleyards, and in April 1951 a deputation met with the Chief Secretary, Mr Dodgshun. Despite an assurance from the Chief Secretary that he had given instructions to the Commissioner of Police that saleyards be strictly supervised and firm action taken against breaches of the law, the League found that some continued to allow poor conditions. They found several instances of cruelty in Dandenong, with large animals frequently trampling on smaller ones, and injured animals not being killed until the end of the day. Underweight calves were illegally being sold to the meat industry, and every day some could be seen injured and dying. Cows were often left unmilked, 'their udders dripping, until they are in agony, so that inexperienced prospective buyers, when buying them for milking, might find that the milk comes easily. No effort is made to check this form of cruelty, which might net extra shillings for a callous owner'. At Warragul it was reported that 'deliberate and unnecessary acts of cruelty go unchecked', and there was no apparent police supervision. Croydon however, had taken some positive steps to ensure that underweight calves were not sold for slaughter but were sold to farmers. Injured animals were destroyed as soon as possible.

The League also investigated shocking conditions in some knackers' yards. The findings were passed on to the Health Department for further investigation.

One of the people who assisted the Anti-Cruelty League was journalist Ronald Hobbs who was Chief of Staff of the *Herald* from 1951 to 1955. He was respected as a journalist of integrity and an article in the *Herald* on 31 March 1956, the day after his death, quoted Mrs Lort Smith as saying that he was a constant fighter against cruelty to animals. When the extensions to the hospital were completed in 1960 one of the operating theatres was named after him.

Mr Ronald Hobbs,
Herald **31 March 1956,**
AWL scrapbook.

As already mentioned, around the mid-1950s the role of the Animal Welfare League shifted from a front-line involvement to one concerned with policy matters and supporting other groups in their campaigns. The role of investigation was taken over entirely by the RSPCA.

The League's constitution did not allow its members to belong to the committees of animal welfare societies, and it was often reluctant to give other animal welfare agencies direct support. When asked to join an organisation the League would almost invariably give a donation rather than any other form of assistance. As an example, when in November 1984 the Australian Animal Protection Society asked for liaison with the League, a donation of $20 was sent.

In December 1979 Sadie Howe attended state parliament with representatives of other animal welfare organisations to discuss the banning of animal traps. Whilst parliament seemed set on banning traps in urban areas, the trapping of rabbits was more problematical. It was decided to sponsor a competition for the design of an alternative trap, but unfortunately after several attempts to interest inventors the matter lapsed.

In May 1981 a coalition was formed to stop live export of animals for slaughter. The Animal Welfare League gave a $10 donation and Sadie Howe, Jan Quintino, Helen Allchin and Phyl Taylor attended a seminar on the subject held by the RSPCA.

In September 1981 it was agreed to donate $20 toward the cost of a campaign against the export of dog pelts which was being organised by the Dalmatian Club of Victoria. The same meeting also approved a $50 donation to a Save the Animals appeal which was being run by the RSPCA. A campaign to prevent the selling of domestic animals at the Queen Victoria Market was coordinated by the Victorian Federation of Animal Welfare Societies and supported by the Animal Welfare League. As a result of their lobbying it was made illegal to sell puppies, dogs, kittens or cats at the market from 1 January 1982.

Another issue which the League pursued around this time was the retailing of Defender snail pellets. It was suggested that a clearer warning about the effects on dogs be put on the packets, and Dr

Lawther also suggested that something be put into the snail bait to make dogs vomit. The manufacturers did act on the first suggestion and said that they would investigate the possibilities of the second.

The League had always been a supporter of the principles of animal liberation, and in response to a request for support received from Animal Liberation in February 1989 the Board agreed to a donation of $1000. This was despite the fact that:

... it had been necessary to remove a group of unruly and noisy animal Liberationists from the waiting room under threat of police action. The group had invaded the Cattery and abused staff regarding stray cats and kittens put to sleep. (Minutes 7 February 1989)

A covering letter was to be sent outlining the League's concern about the demonstration. It was discovered, following a question by Pat Patience two years later, that the money and therefore the letter had, inadvertently, not been sent.

There were some issues to which the League was sympathetic but reluctant to commit itself too openly for fear of attracting adverse publicity. One such example was a wildlife rescue mission in the duck-shooting area. In March 1994 the Board agreed to a request by Steven Isaacs for a loan of one of the hospital ambulances on condition that the hospital name was masked and that it attract no adverse publicity. It also provided first aid equipment and agreed that hospital rosters could be rearranged to allow staff to go to the area.

The Companion Animals Report was tabled in parliament on 1 March 1988. The League was represented at the public hearing on 6 June 1988 by Sadie Howe, Ron Joyce and Jan Fattohi. That month Sadie Howe reported that the League's submission had been very well received by the committee. The committee findings were to be presented to parliament later that year but in fact the legislation was not passed until several years later.

This Bill was moved by the state Labor Party and agreement and support was forthcoming from all animal welfare groups that had been involved in discussions and working parties organised by the Ministry of Agriculture. One of the recommendations was the compulsory registration of cats; to encourage cats to be desexed it was recommended that the registration fee for an entire cat should be 200% that of a desexed cat. However, there was a lot of misleading information being disseminated about the Bill in an attempt to have it fail, including the false information that a cat registration fee would be $200. Various lobby groups were involved including those with vested interests such as pet food manufacturers. The Liberal and National Parties were threatening to block the legislation.

In April 1992 Dr Graeme Smith from the Lost Dogs' Home addressed a meeting of the Board with details of the campaign which animal welfare agencies were conducting to gain politicians' support for the passing of the bill. One suggestion was that all stray animals should be taken to the offices of politicians to alert them to the size of the problem.

The League helped support the campaign by contributing toward an advertisement in the *Herald Sun* newspaper, and in May 1992 Ian Dodd and Ron Joyce attended a rally of supporters of the Bill on the steps of Parliament House. There had been several speakers including the Minister for Agriculture, Mr Baker. Hospital staff also attended with the ambulance.

Campaigning for tax deductibility status has been an on-going issue for the League and some other animal welfare bodies for the past seventy years. Campaigning has taken two forms – lobbying politicians, and highlighting the difficulties of non-tax-deductibility through the press. A few examples are given here.

On 5 April 1949 the Board decided to write to Harold Holt asking him to take up the issue, which he agreed to do in a reply dated 26 April. He had asked the Treasurer to include a suitable amendment to the sales tax legislation to grant the desired relief when the act was next before parliament. The effort came to nothing. The Board next approached the Prime Minister, Mr Menzies, in August 1959 but with the same negative response.

In May 1959 Board member Joan Dickson wrote a personal letter to the Treasurer, Harold Holt, stating a strong case for federal support. The hospital was operating at a loss of £5000 per annum despite a state government grant of £500. He replied that 'it is a very good thing that we have in our community warm-hearted and public-spirited citizens who are prepared to give their time and energy to such a worthy cause' and promised to raise the matter with the Commissioner of Taxation. The response was that tax deductibility could not be allowed.

In the early 1990s the Animal Welfare League of New South Wales asked for other animal welfare bodies to join in establishing a National Secretariat of Animal Welfare Leagues, whose main aim was to lobby parliament to grant tax exemption. This move followed advice which the secretary of the NSW league had received from Paul Keating, who was then Treasurer, that any approach could only be made on a national basis.

In June 1991 the League received an invitation to attend a meeting in Sydney to discuss the formation of a national body comprising the animal welfare leagues of each state, but the Board was very reluctant to become involved. It was finally persuaded by being told, in January 1992, that all the states except Victoria had agreed to a meeting which, to make it easier for the League to attend, would be held in Victoria. The outcome was an agreement for a loose association of the states, but the establishment of a national secretariat with its own office was not considered necessary because of the costs involved. Meetings were to be held approximately twice a year or when necessary. Venues and the necessary administrative arrangements were to be shared by each state in rotation. The travel costs were to be shared equally.

A meeting was held in Sydney on 29 August 1992 and was attended by Ian Dodd and John Honey. Ian Dodd reported back to the Board that the meeting had been most informative, and there appeared to be a good case for a national body which would benefit all states by way of tax exemptions for donations, and on the sale of goods, and by providing a single voice for animal welfare nationally. Each state would retain its autonomy and articles of association were to be drawn up by a member of the NSW league who was a solicitor. A draft copy of these articles was received in June 1993 and a further meeting, held in Queensland on 27 November, was attended by the hospital secretary Susie Palmer, and Alan Lawther. A constitution was to be drawn up and the proposed annual fee was to be no more than $2000.

Dr Jacqui Moore with dog, *Sunday Herald Sun,* **23 April 2000,**
Photo: Rob Leeson.

It was suggested that the secretary and president should be chosen from different states and that the positions should rotate every two years. In January 1995 Susie Palmer was appointed secretary.

At the December Board meeting Susie Palmer reported on a successful annual general meeting of the national league which she had recently attended in Queensland. The animal food manufacturer Uncle Ben's, had offered to finance the tax deductibility campaign, and later in 1998 Uncle Ben's briefed a professional lobbyist to take the matter further.

Gradually different states indicated their unwillingness to support the national body because the lack of success did not justify the high costs involved. At this time there was a suggestion that the body should continue to meet informally – some of the states were already meeting regularly because of their common interest in running cat and dog shelters – but nothing came of it and the national league petered out.

In the meantime the League in Victoria continued to lobby on its own behalf. Hopes that the government would make the necessary amendments to the legislation were dashed early in 1998 when Mr Webb was told in a letter from the Assistant Treasurer that this would not occur. Attempts at employing a professional lobbyist also met with no success, and in September 1999 Alan Lawther told the Board that he had been advised that 'we have no hope at this present time'.

A further publicity campaign took place in April 2000, shortly before the hospital moved into its new premises and the League continues to use every possible opportunity to lobby for the necessary change in legislation. In April 2000 the *Sunday Herald Sun* ran an editorial supporting tax exemption and an article by Julie Hosking describing the work of the hospital and its financial plight.

13 An after-word

The challenges which faced the Board when the Lort Smith Animal Hospital opened in 1936 are essentially the same challenges that the Board grapples with today. They will doubtless remain for as long as the hospital continues to live up to its ideals.

There is a strange paradox in the staff profile of the hospital. It has a core of loyal and dedicated staff whose years of service parallel those of earlier times. Twelve staff members out of a total of approximately eighty have been employed for more than ten years, and some for considerably longer. Joan Sturzaker was appointed in 1977, Steven Isaacs in 1979, Vladimir Kogan in 1981 and John Honey in 1982. Dr José Sequeira worked at the hospital for seventeen-and-a-half years. Yet the average length of service does not reflect this trend. Attracting and retaining appropriate staff has always been a problem. Financial rewards are evidently only part of the problem, although perhaps a significant part.

In periods of strong leadership, where staff have felt that the Board and managers listened to and supported them, the morale has improved, but like a yo-yo, there have been periods of staff satisfaction and stability alternating with periods of uncertainty and sometimes crisis.

An ongoing dilemma for the Board is how to continue to be faithful to the charter of the League and yet remain economically viable. To ensure its long-term survival the hospital must, as far as possible, operate so that it does not make a loss. It needs to attract fee-paying clients who can subsidise those of limited financial means who qualify for discounted rates. Otherwise it has to depend on donations and legacies and fundraising activities all of which depend on the goodwill of the public, which cannot be guaranteed, particularly in times of economic uncertainty.

A senior vet made this comment about how he sees the hospital's future:

Lort Smith is struggling with its identity and the type of service that it is to offer to what range of clients ... I believe that if we were able to expand our service to attract the general pet owning population we would be able to increase revenue and effect both the above. Unfortunately there is a lack of enthusiasm to move from the status quo (what we have been doing for years). It is my grave concern that if there is not a radical change in the path followed by the Lort Smith Animal Hospital that we may be in a situation soon where the financial pressures are unbearable and I am concerned that the response will be to cut staff. I believe that the future of the Lort Smith Animal Hospital requires a large shift in philosophy and that needs to be a shared vision of all from the Board to the kennels because it will require all to push in the same direction at the same time to make that happen.

Management of investments and property has been one of the strengths of the League since the mid-1960s. The Board is well endowed with financial know-how and is supported by a highly skilled finance manager which is particularly important in times of global economic uncertainty. It also has the services of some highly experienced vets to keep abreast of the latest in veterinary practice. What it needs above all is the vision and will to resolve its current difficulties.

The hospital is faced with a dilemma. The more treatment it provides, whether free, subsidised or charged at the standard hospital rates, the more money it loses because the real cost of treatment is high. The forecast trading loss for the year 2002/3 is $2 million.

The hospital is fortunate because its demonstrated commitment to the welfare of animals and their owners does continue to attract donations and bequests which allow it to continue its work. But the struggle to raise funds is made harder by the fact that supporters are unable to claim donations as tax deductions. This is a challenge which the League, and other animal welfare groups, continues to fight.

Reading through the records of the hospital's history it has at times been difficult to foresee how it could survive. How could the Board consistently ignore the highly rational and experienced advice of its honorary treasurer in the 1940s and its financial advisory committee in the 1950s and '60s when they were threatened with possible financial disaster and bankruptcy? The message of St Paul of the importance of the three virtues of faith, hope and charity comes to mind. Today charity is likely to be interpreted as compassion and empathy and all the actions which follow from such emotions.

Dr Judith Slocombe, President Animal Welfare League of Victoria 2003, *Photo: Melbourne Business School.*

Dr Judith Slocombe, a locum at the Lort Smith Animal Hospital for several years, was mentioned in chapter ten. She was the 2001 Telstra Australian Businesswoman of the Year, and was the guest speaker at the League's June 2002 annual general meeting. As part of her talk she discussed the different styles of leadership of men and women. She spoke of the masculine leadership style of today as strong, powerful, assertive, charismatic and dominant whereas women provided a style of leadership which was more caring, collaborative and uniting – words which she summed up with the word 'empathy'. This characteristic, the ability to enter into the feelings of others, is one of the leadership strengths of the Lort Smith Animal Hospital and, according to Judith Slocombe, 'people find empathy waiting for them' when they visit the hospital.

The new General Manager, Peter Brown, who took over the position in February 2002, has a strong vision for the hospital's future. The innovations he has brought to the hospital during his first year include:

• An Ambassador program which aims to recruit well known personalities from a variety of different interests and backgrounds to actively promote the work of the hospital. To date Peter Hitchener, newsreader from Channel 9, and the flamboyant Melbourne entertainer Roland Rocchiccioli have accepted this role with enthusiasm. A public relations firm Socom Response, have undertaken to assist in establishing this program on a pro-bono basis, and also to assist with other projects aimed at raising the profile of the hospital.

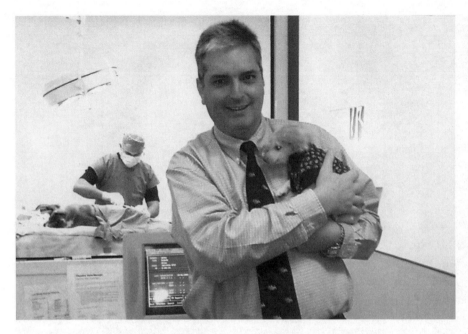

Mr Peter Brown,
General Manager,
*Photo: Lort Smith
Hospital.*

- Members of Leadership Victoria's Community Skillsbank Leadership program are assisting the hospital to develop a strategic plan aimed at ensuring the financial viability of the hospital. Four people have volunteered to work on a pro-bono basis: Neil McCarthy, Ricci Meldrum, Paul Higgins and Lex McArthur.
- A Community Arts Project, with support from the City of Melbourne. This is embarking on an ambitious undertaking - a large mural focussing on people and pets which will cover the north wall of the hospital enclosure.
- There are also plans for the hospital to take a lead role in extending the Aboriginal Community Dog Health program which is run in the Northern Territory into East Timor, and active measures are underway to gather sponsorship and material assistance to enable this venture to materialise. It is hoped that the hospital can also play an active role in the training of vets from East Timor.

At his first annual general meeting in May 2002 Peter talked about how he saw the role and the future of the hospital. He stressed the League's interest in the social aspects of its service which he believed

Mrs Patricia Williams and her dog Skye,
Herald Sun 28 May 2002, Photo: Andrew Batsch.

distinguishes it from other animal welfare organisations. He emphasised the need for collaboration with social welfare agencies working with people as well as other animal welfare organisations, and he stressed the need for the League to develop strategic partnerships.

He concluded with a story which, as a lecturer in wildlife management, he had told to his students when asked 'how can we possibly make a difference when so many animal species are threatened with extinction?' Following a heavy storm a woman was walking along a beach and found thousands of starfish washed up upon the shore, stranded and dying. So she started to throw them back into the sea. As she did this a man walked towards her and asked what she was doing and how could she possibly help to make a difference since the task was clearly too great. She looked at the man and slowly bent down and picked up one of the starfish writhing on the sand and gently threw it back to the sea – 'Well I made a difference to that one...' And that is what the Lort Smith Animal Hospital does – it makes a difference in the individual lives of many animals and their owners.

A recent example of how the hospital continues to make a difference and remain true to its charter of not turning away animals requiring treatment was well publicised in the *Herald* in May 2002 under the heading 'Dying pet refused care'. Mrs Patricia Williams desperately tried to find a vet willing to treat her severely ill dog Skye when it had swallowed rodent poison. Every one she contacted asked for evidence of her ability to pay – and temporary financial difficulties meant that she was unable to provide this evidence. After four hours on the phone, and requests for help from more than a dozen vets, the Lort Smith Animal Hospital agreed to give the dog the treatment it needed and to allow Patricia to pay off her bill-which amounted to $350 – in regular instalments.

A footnote to this story is the generosity of the public who donated more than enough money to the hospital to cover the cost of Skye's treatment, and all the donations were made on the condition of anonymity. It is because of the kindness of strangers that the hospital survives.

Bibliography

Australian Dictionary of Biography, Melbourne University Press 1966

'Battle of the Bolt', Margaret Hazzard, in *Parade*, June 1974.

Newspapers:

Melbourne Truth

The Age

The Argus

The Australasian

Herald

Herald Sun

The Sun

Pix

Table Talk

Woman's Day

Unpublished materials:

Minute books and various materials held by the Lort Smith Animal Hospital.

Index